Praise for *Adapt*

'How extraordinarily apt is the title *Adapt*? Adapt it is, to digitisation, to skills shortages, to the rise of AI. And *Adapt* is so versatile for it is a strategy, a philosophy, a state of mind. Clarke's *Adapt* is a masterpiece in brevity and insight that is as bold and impactful as its title suggests.'
Bernard Salt AM, The Demographics Group

'A masterclass in resilience, showing us how to embrace change, not fear it. This is a bold call to action for anyone feeling unsettled about the future of work.'
Dr Catherine Ball, Scientific Futurist

'Andrea's simple yet powerful approach to adaptive leadership has empowered countless Rio Tinto employees to confidently navigate the future, both as professionals and as an organisation.'
Brendan Howard, Rio Tinto

'A must read for anyone ready to stop reacting and start shaping their future.'
Natalie Slessor, CBRE

'*Adapt* demystifies change, giving us the confidence to tackle it head on, to embrace and welcome it willingly into a new way of living a full life.'
Kim Mills, Australian Department of Defence

'While a reversion to the safety of the past is appealing, as leaders we must evolve and guide our people and our organisations into a new future. In *Adapt*, Andrea gives you the gift of clarity – a moment to pause and reflect on how you will help shape the future.'
Shamal Dass, UNSW Business School

'What sets *Adapt* apart is its focus on action. Instead of endless theorising, planning and overthinking, Andrea empowers us to simply *do*. If you're stuck in analysis paralysis, this book is the lever you need to start anticipating what's next and being an active player in this non-stop universe of transformation.'
Emile Perrine, Global Transformation Expert

'*Adapt* is a blueprint to help readers shape what comes next in their own life. This book's four principles are a compass for anyone reckoning with change at any stage in their life. And it is spot-on, audacious guidance on how to embrace change *on purpose*.'
Yvette Gonzalez, Human Health & Climate Researcher

'This book doesn't just preach adaptability – it equips you with the tools to gain the agency to thrive amid chaos. It's a must read for 21st-century leaders and anyone who wants to lead with foresight, confidently embrace the unpredictable future, and harness the new superpowers technology affords us.'
Sami Mäkeläinen, Global Foresight Expert

Adapt

Mastering change
in four steps

Andrea
Clarke

**SIMON &
SCHUSTER**

New York · Amsterdam/Antwerp · London · Toronto · Sydney · New Delhi

ADAPT: MASTERING CHANGE IN FOUR STEPS
First published in Australia in 2025 by
Simon & Schuster (Australia) Pty Limited
Level 4, 32 York St, Sydney NSW 2000

10 9 8 7 6 5 4 3 2 1

New York Amsterdam/Antwerp London Toronto Sydney New Delhi
Visit our website at www.simonandschuster.com.au

© Andrea Clarke 2025

All rights reserved. No part of this publication may be reproduced, stored in a retrieval system, or transmitted in any form or by any means, electronic, mechanical, photocopying, recording or otherwise, without prior permission of the publisher.

Every effort has been made to contact all copyright owners prior to publication of *Adapt* to ensure that their contribution is properly acknowledged. Where we have been unable, despite our best endeavours, to make contact we would welcome hearing from anyone concerned, so that we may include an appropriate acknowledgement in any reprints.

A catalogue record for this book is available from the National Library of Australia

ISBN: 9781761632433

Cover design: Sarah Cronin, Bluehaus Designs
Typeset by Midland Typesetters, Australia
Printed and bound in Australia by Griffin Press

The paper this book is printed on is certified against the Forest Stewardship Council® Standards. Griffin Press holds chain of custody certification SCS-COC-001185. FSC® promotes environmentally responsible, socially beneficial and economically viable management of the world's forests.

Contents

Foreword by Dominic Price, Work Futurist at Atlassian — vii

Introduction Be the pilot, not the passenger — 1

Fundamentals

1 A new way — 15
2 Modern success metrics — 31

The four principles

3 Engage — 55
4 Accept — 89
5 Activate — 117
6 Release — 141

What's next?

7 The energy for change — 165
8 Making sense and moving on — 191

Conclusion True north versus magnetic north — 207
Acknowledgements — 215
References — 217
Index — 219
About the author — 226

Foreword

The truth about change

For the past twenty years, leaders and workers have been sold the myth of transformation – big, shiny, expensive transformations that promise to fix everything. I've seen it time and again: companies pay millions for an agile transformation, a cultural transformation or a digital overhaul. They expect that at the end of this 18- or 24-month journey, they'll cut a ribbon, take a bow and, boom, they're transformed.

But here's the truth: in the time it takes to complete that transformation, the world has already changed. Leaders often come to me frustrated that they've gone through these massive changes only to find that they're still behind. And here's the point – they've been sold the wrong idea. Change isn't a one-time event. The world keeps moving, and if you think you can buy change, cut the ribbon and be done with it, you're in for an expensive wake-up call. The world keeps shifting, and those old leadership behaviours and strategies from the '80s, '90s and early 2000s just don't work anymore. Leadership in 2024 is about being relevant, and relevance means you have to keep learning and changing as the world changes around you.

You cannot outsource personal change

Real transformation starts from within. So many organisations try to change by hiring consultants, updating their processes or installing new technology only to find that the core of their business – the behaviours, the leadership practices, the values – remains the same. And so nothing really changes. The leaders who get it, who truly understand how to lead through change, don't just change the tools they use; they change *how they behave*. It's not enough to change the language or the technology – you have to change the way you think, the way you lead and the way you relate to your people. That's where real transformation happens. When leaders take responsibility for their own growth and adaptability, that's when the organisation changes. You can't outsource that. You have to own it. And when you do, when you lead by example, the people around you start to change. That's the ripple effect of true leadership. But most leaders don't do this. They think they can buy transformation, but they haven't invested in their own growth. They haven't developed the adaptability muscle. They haven't learned how to change from within. And that's why so many organisations and people find themselves stuck, even after the 'big transformation' that has cost the business tens of millions of dollars.

Foreword

Chopping down trees versus finding fertile ground

One of the biggest challenges I see with leaders today is what I like to call 'chopping down trees'. It's a simple metaphor for being stuck in the daily grind, constantly solving problems that feel urgent, but never making time to think about the future. You know the feeling. Your inbox is overflowing, your calendar's packed with back-to-back meetings, and your to-do list is more like a never-ending playlist that you dread to look at. So you spend your days chopping down trees – putting out fires, managing crises and handling whatever comes your way.

And here's the thing: chopping down trees is necessary. It keeps things running. But here's the real issue: if all you ever do is chop down trees, eventually you'll run out of forest. Sure, you'll fix today's problems, but you won't have planted any seeds for tomorrow's growth. And when the forest is gone? You'll be stuck, with no way to move forward. Planting seeds is about creating space for exploration and future thinking. So how much of your time is spent chopping down trees, and how much is spent looking for fertile ground? How much energy are you putting into nurturing the seeds that could grow into tomorrow's innovations? Because if you're not making time to plant those seeds now, you're setting yourself up for failure later. It's not a matter of *if* you'll run out of trees, it's *when*.

Here's the thing, though: most people I talk to know this. They *get* it. They understand the importance of thinking about the future. But when I ask them why they aren't doing it, the answer is almost always the same: 'I don't have time.' The day-to-day grind is relentless, and it feels impossible to carve out space to think about tomorrow when today's fires are burning out of control. But here's what I tell them: if you don't make time to plant seeds now, you'll be forced to make time later when you've run out of trees – and by then, it might be too late. That's the confronting reality of leadership today. We're so focused on solving today's problems that we often neglect the future, and by the time we realise it, we're already behind. The challenge is finding the balance between the short-term demands of leadership and the long-term need to stay ahead of the curve. You *have* to carve out the mental space to plant seeds for the future, even when the pressure of the present feels overwhelming.

The cost of not changing

We need to plant seeds because the cost of *not* changing is far greater than the discomfort of adapting. It's easy to stick to the old ways of doing things, especially when they've worked in the past. But here's the hard truth: if you're not moving forward, you're static, and the cost of staying still is massive. You might not feel it today, but over time it adds up. You become less relevant, less competitive, and eventually you get left behind. That's the real danger – not just failure, but irrelevance. And yet so many leaders resist change because they're afraid of the discomfort it brings. They don't want to experiment. They don't want to fail. But here's the thing: the cost of not changing is far greater than the risk of failure. Every failed experiment teaches you something. Every time you take a risk, you learn.

What's important here is that change only happens when we actually do it.

Understanding change means doing it

We can't understand change just because we've read the right books, attended the right conferences and listened to the right podcasts. Many people can talk about agility, transformation and innovation with ease. But here's the truth: understanding change isn't the same as doing it. Knowing about change is one thing, but actually leading through it is another. It's easy to talk about change in theory, but until you start experimenting, until you start taking risks, you haven't really got it.

Too many leaders intellectualise change. They spend time reading, studying and thinking about it, but they never take the necessary steps to act. They don't experiment. They don't try new things. And so they stay stuck. The leaders who excel today are the ones who take action. They're not just talking about change – they're living it. They're experimenting, taking risks and learning from their failures. They're talking about it. They understand that doing the same thing over and over won't pay off.

Let's form a 'do-ocracy' movement around modern work and find things today that build a better future. I'm not saying kill your dreams – just make them more realistic by taking ownership of the steps to create that better future, and putting them into action. We won't look back and say 'AI, crypto and 5G really saved us as a society', so let's get on with creating our future on purpose, and not by accident.

Future-proofing versus firefighting

If you've picked up this book, then you're at least a little curious about your role in change. We've all been there. We've all been in a position where we felt we were just chopping down trees. All we could see was trees. So now is the time to ask yourself: am I happy doing this? And what do I have control over? What is within my power, my ability to influence change? We have more personal agency than we know – and this is where we need to find things to subtract. What if you chopped fewer trees – would anyone notice? If they wouldn't, maybe that's a sign you are overinvesting in your job. If you pulled back a little bit and gave yourself three hours a week to invest in doing it better in the future – in future-proofing rather than firefighting – would that give you some benefit? Absolutely.

Give it a red-hot go

Taking a moment to think about how many trees you are chopping down versus how many seeds you are planting is a good start. And *Adapt* will provoke you to examine your current relationship with change. But here's the thing: don't just read it. *Do something.* Experiment. Apply the ideas in this book. Take action. It's not about doing everything perfectly – it's about starting small and building from there. The cost of not changing is too high. You have more control over your future than you realise, and it starts with taking ownership. You can't outsource your growth. You can't buy transformation. You have to own it.

Foreword

So take the first step. Start experimenting. Start adapting. The future is coming, whether you're ready or not.

And who better to meet you where you are today than Andrea Clarke? In 2019, the former journalist interviewed me for her first, award-winning career book, *Future Fit: How to Stay Relevant and Competitive in the Future of Work* – a book that has encouraged countless readers to go all in on owning their leadership journey. Through her continued commitment to the growth of herself and others, Andrea has offered us an equally relevant title in *Adapt*. Here is a book that wraps personal stories around practical advice on how to understand what's changing around you, upgrade your ability to adapt, and ultimately have more influence over the way change lands around you. This is how we can feel more confident about the future, build a future 'on purpose' and encourage others to do the same.

I say, give it a red-hot go.

Dominic Price

Introduction

Be the pilot, not the passenger

'Pan-pan-pan!'

'Find me an airstrip to land,' was the loud and clear direction given to my fourteen-year-old sister, as my father handed her a map. We didn't need an explanation; we knew what was going on.

We had just had an engine failure.

Dad was piloting his four-seat, single-engine Cessna 210 with his three young girls on board. On this particular afternoon, we were on a routine trip from a cotton farm outside of Moree in Northern New South Wales, headed 500 kilometres north-east to the Southport Flying Club on the Gold Coast. We were at 9000 feet and running at 170 knots (about 300 kilometres per hour) when the Cessna lost power. As three unruly young girls, it was standard for us to be brought into line with one snap command from Dad. But this line had an extra punch.

'Pan-pan-pan' stands for 'possible assistance needed' and is one step before 'mayday'. Pilots use this to signal that an aircraft is experiencing a problem, but that there is no immediate danger.

Dad radioed this in and stated his intention to land. This allowed the Brisbane radio tower to alert a nearby twin-engine aircraft, which diverted to our position. He was instructed to keep a visual on us and relay any 'information' back to Brisbane. In this instance, 'information' was code for 'if we crashed'.

What happened next was a pure play in adaptive leadership. In a calm and procedural manner, Dad handed Megan the map while he flew the plane and figured out what was next.

He managed to partially restart the engine, but it was running with significantly less power.

Dad knew that with less than 50 per cent engine power at that altitude, we had a range of 30 kilometres. I could see that he was switching focus with intent: looking down at his instruments and then looking up and out at our position, scanning the horizon. We glided for 9000 feet and when we were 2000 feet away from the dirt airstrip in front of us, Dad tilted the nose down. And when I say 'down', I mean on a very steep angle, looking directly towards the ground. We had one shot at making this landing strip. And we did.

As soon as we came to a stop – which is definitely more violent in a small plane than a commercial plane – Dad scrambled out and blasted open the engine cover, trying to confirm an explanation for the midair freefall.

Introduction

Training for change

By the day of this incident, Dad had spent 3000-plus hours in light aircraft and helicopters. He had more hours logged in the simulator and alongside an instructor, whose job it was to test his limits in live, midair drills, where the engine was deliberately switched off. So, in some form, his brain had been here before. Through training for change he had rewired his brain to consider untested scenarios, so his response to a crisis was to counter the panic with process.

The culprit on the day he was flying with us turned out to be the exhaust distributor. According to his logbook, it was the very same part that had rotted through several years earlier, causing a drastic loss of power on take-off from Hamilton Island. The loss of power was so significant that the aircraft couldn't gain any lift, and was on the verge of stalling. The only option was to prepare to ditch. He instructed his co-pilot to watch the instruments while he looked around to see where they could put the aircraft down. He somehow managed to slowly circle the crippled Cessna and land on the airstrip, but not before he told passengers to open the doors so they could exit the plane without obstruction when they hit the water. The passenger in the back, John Beale ('Bealey' to his mates), was a long-time friend of Dad's. The incident caused Bealey so much distress that he suffered a heart attack later that day, when the group was airborne for a second time. With a medical emergency onboard, Dad declared a mayday 50 kilometres north of Townsville and screamed towards the runway at 180 knots.

The miracle for Bealey was that Dad's co-pilot was also a surgeon and had his medical kit on hand. Dr Peter Drum is the only reason Bealey is alive today.

Look up and out

When we speak about it now, Dad brushes it off with the nonchalance of a 78-year-old who's been around the block. And of course he does: part of his job as a pilot is to respond effectively to these moments that he has trained for. To him, it was a simple act of applying knowledge in a scenario that had been rehearsed many times. But I see it very differently. It's only now, in my late forties, that I realise this was a defining moment in shaping the way I wanted to move around this big, wide world. I saw so much more in that moment. I saw a highly effective practice in adaptive leadership. I saw his preparation and training play out and pay off in real time. I saw someone 'looking up and out' to understand what was changing. I saw a composed leader exercising live adaptability in a situation that a less experienced pilot may not have recovered.

It was an early and profound lesson about the role of adaptability in life; this was a skill that was fundamental to confidently handling moments of ambiguity. When things are moving fast and we need to respond swiftly to an untested scenario, it's not our IQ or EQ (emotional intelligence) that we reach for, it's our ability to adapt – it's our AQ that we rely on. It's our adaptability quotient. And AQ is not only about reacting and responding, it's about actively shaping what comes next.

Introduction

Watching the way Dad handled this midair engine failure anchored in me a deep and lasting truth: if I could practise the adaptive principles that saved us that day, I could be a pilot and not a passenger on my own little life journey. If I could always do my best to 'look up and out' over my own personal dashboard, and anticipate change instead of waiting for it to happen to me, I would have a better chance at being the author of my own life script instead of being an extra in someone else's. I could use the map he showed us to go wherever I wanted to.

As a 12-year-old, I saw Dad's response as the *only* way to approach life. Disruption comes at us in many forms; it has a speed, a scale and a direction. We can sit idle and be a victim of it, or we can play an active part in how it lands around us. This is what I've always wanted for myself.

And I want the same for you.

I share this story with you because although we may not be going to work every day worried about engine failure, many of us are waking up every day facing our own versions of untested scenarios. We're facing more change, more often – on diminished reserves and with more distractions than ever. And the lesson for my 12-year-old self is still relevant today, and relevant for each of us: when we are an active player in the process of change, we create a new sense of stability for ourselves that is grounded in deep resilience, personal agency and alignment with our true self.

When we shift from being someone who is waiting for change to happen to us to someone who pre-empts change, we reposition our role in the process. We interrupt our default relationship with change. We empower ourselves to anticipate challenges and opportunities, make thoughtful decisions, let go of outdated beliefs and create a life aligned with our values and aspirations. In the 2010 journal article, 'Psychological Flexibility as a Fundamental Aspect of Health', authors Kashdan and Rottenberg noted that people who are more adaptable tend to report higher levels of happiness and wellbeing. This makes sense, because a core component of adaptability is having a flexible and resilient mindset that is open to change. This psychological flexibility plays a foundational role in how we handle the uncertainties of life, which is why an adaptive mindset is not only helpful to pilots, but helpful to us every single day, as we wake up to live and work in a world that feels as though it's picking up speed.

Life feels faster, but not necessarily happier
I know it's not just me. I feel like I've been on a merry-go-round that broke down for a year. After spinning at a reasonable pace, we collectively came to a screaming halt and evacuated the ride to sit on the grass for a while. And when the motor cranked up again, we each got back in the saddle and adjusted our reins, reacquainting ourselves with the feel of it all as the ride gradually picked up speed. After a few false starts and splutters, the engine – fuelled by artificial intelligence, escalated political

Introduction

discourse, emerging identity politics and social media – started accelerating at a pace we didn't know existed. The merry-go-round is now spinning faster than it did before. And now, we're far more exhausted than we were before March 2020. And we want off this ride. Or at the very least, we want control of the switch.

And why wouldn't we? In a very short window, our traditional sense of 'work' has undergone a radical transformation, leaving our lives – and the way we live them – completely up for renewal. We don't want to feel like we're being left behind, but at the same time we don't know how to keep up. We're also feeling a sense of disquiet and dis-ease about the future. As my friend Dr Catherine Ball says, 'We've not had a funeral for whatever it was we experienced through the pandemic. We haven't stopped and grieved whatever it was that we lost in the fire.'

The official term is 'social acceleration', and it impacts every part of our lives. Faster technology, faster communication, faster production and consumption cycles. Our social norms, values and relationships are changing more rapidly than ever. What once took generations to evolve can now change within a few years, or even months, thanks to social media, hyper-connectivity and Insta-driven cultural trends.

German sociologist Hartmut Rosa highlights the paradox of this acceleration in his 2013 book, *Social Acceleration: A New Theory of Modernity*. He explains that being driven to achieve more in less time often results in feelings of alienation, burnout and a lack of fulfilment. The constant push to keep up with the accelerating demands of modern life can erode the quality of social relationships, community bonds and individual well-being. It pushes us further back when we think we're driving forward.

The retreat is real

For many of us, the workplace is where we are confronted most frequently with these accelerations. Untested scenarios are playing out in the loosening up of professional boundaries, the shifting power dynamic between the worker and workplace, and clashing of expectations around how we deliver work – while at the same time, trying to figure out exactly how artificial intelligence will impact us.

There are new, undefined rules of engagement emerging across the workplace – and they're making many of us nervous. So much so that we're not only retreating back to a safe place, we're locking the door behind us.

And what we're taking into that safe place is significant. As we quietly step back, we're taking with us the opportunity to exercise creative leadership, promote innovation, strengthen connections and adapt effectively to change.

This has been clear in a sample executive opinion poll I ran with 40 leaders across a number of industry sectors, where people volunteered that they feel, among other things, that 'taking a different [less bold] approach to leadership' is the only option to reduce any kind of personal risk. The sentiment was summed up in these responses: 'I'm a people leader who doesn't want to lead people anymore', and 'I try not to be creative'.

And here lies the problem: we're quietly stepping back to a safe and neutral place – when there has never been a more dangerous time to be neutral on change.

Let go of stability

Layered around the workplace is a less visible tension: it feels as though there's an underlying strain between what we're experiencing (change overwhelm) and how we're encouraged to deal with it (find stability).

Why is this? Because the social narrative about change relies on a script from previous generations, who lived in distinctly different eras. That script encourages us to resist change, steer a safe course and do things as they've always been done. Change is seen as a threat to our life script and a shadow that undermines our stability.

It's a strong and consistent theme across our culture. We see it in the workplace, where many CEOs are giving orders from a 1980s handbook.

We see it at home as well, when our extended families gather around a table – perhaps a birthday, graduation or holiday celebration that brings everyone together. Senior members of the family make comments that represent the beliefs of an older generation who are entirely removed from the challenges of the present day. The subtext of the script implicitly reads: don't rock the boat, stay in a secure job, stay together for the kids, pay your bills in person. Look how it's worked for us!

So, it seems like it's time to set fire to the old script. It's time to let go of the fundamental belief that we should pursue stability at all costs. Maybe we need to pause again. Maybe we need a new relationship with change.

A simple proposition

So here is my simple proposition: if we want to feel more aligned with ourselves, be healthier, happier and have a greater sense of agency over our life regardless of how fast the world is spinning, we need to be in a continual conversation with change. We need to understand how it happens, see it as a force for constant growth and shift our mindset from responding and reacting to anticipating and influencing change. And why now, why should we prioritise the ideas in this book today, this week or this year? Because I believe that we are currently in a window of opportunity to make small moves that could change our long game. We have a few years of distance from the global pause in 2020, where we've perhaps made short-term adaptations in response to how we live and work. We now sit in a personal 'medium-term re-ordering' phase of the timeline, before our own norms stabilise for the long term. This is why *now* is the time to be decisive; now is the time to take a position on how we're going to lead ourselves and others, to double down on the work that needs to be done. Even if it's in small ways. I want to offer up some ideas that help you feel relaxed about the future and find a new sense of stability that you can rely on and return to.

Introduction

The four basic principles of *Adapt*

The ideas that have driven my life decisions, and inevitably intersected with my leadership practice, have been led by these questions: how can I help leaders tactically develop their AQ to be better prepared for change, to see it coming, and to shape the way it lands around them?

Since 2018, I have been working with leadership cohorts around the world on this one specific objective: helping people adopt simple high-AQ habits that become part of their daily leadership practice. The more time passes, the more I believe these habits are required for anyone who prioritises self-leading across any aspect of their life.

In these pages, I'll share with you what I've shared with hundreds of teams across multiple markets who are facing paradigm shifts in the way they do business. Through these four principles, I hope that you will discover a new way to think about how to be an active player in your own transformation, or perhaps the transformation of your business, community or family.

Adapt is founded on four principles:
1. **Engage** with the signals of change.
2. **Accept** what's changing.
3. **Activate** your optimism for the new.
4. **Release** what's holding you back.

I have three simple objectives with this book. First, to help you examine your current relationship with change: are you a pilot or a passenger in it? Second, to recognise the role of personal agency: are you acting as an effective agent for yourself? And finally, to provoke you to consider a new way of thinking about what's changing both around you and inside of you. To help you understand how change happens, and the small, safe moves we can make to pre-empt, practise and prepare for it. And to help you understand how you can turn uncertainty into inspired action.

The opportunity for you to adapt

As a facilitator, friend and author, I only share ideas, principles, advice and frameworks that work for me personally, that I have applied to my own life and that have inspired me to turn uncertainty into action. I have repeatedly tested and trusted the four principles of *Adapt* through triaging my own major career transitions – using them both as a life raft and as an anchor to create meaningful change completely aligned with my version of success. When I have shared this with leaders and learners around the world, the outcomes have been remarkable. So here is your opportunity to adapt. As I say to all learners, take what works for you and perhaps leave the rest for someone else. And wherever possible, look for ways to be the pilot, not the passenger, along the way.

Part 1

Fundamentals

1

A new way

New rules of engagement

'One of the most stressful things you can do to a group of human beings is to put them in a room and expect them to work together – but not give them any rules,' says my close friend Alicia Stephenson, who also happens to be a former training officer in the Australian Defence Force, a Telstra Business Award Winner and the CEO of Workforce Dynamics, a group that helps interpret and build better behaviours across global organisations. We were talking about the endless people-related struggles that many are having as the workplace changes.

'Imagine we're sitting beside a pool at a hotel,' she continues. 'We know that getting naked and jumping into the pool is against the rules. We can't see those rules explained anywhere, but we know they are the unspoken rules, and those rules make us comfortable and safe. Now say we locked everyone in here. Over time, we would slowly see the behavioural boundaries stripped away. Some people would really loosen up and it would freak everybody out. If you apply the same theory to the workplace, stripping away the boundaries, you'll see everyone retreat back behind a safe, closed door. And this is exactly what is happening.'

We should not downplay the erosion of professional boundaries that was catalysed by the pandemic, and the way we are being affected by this. Remote work blurred the lines between personal and professional life, leaving many employees unsure of how to behave in this new, boundaryless environment. In the past, visible signs – such as dress codes and hierarchical structures – provided clear cues on how to act professionally. Today, those cues have largely disappeared, leaving people to constantly test and adjust their behaviour, which is exhausting.

Many of us can relate to this, particularly if we're only in the workplace a few days a week, and the office is only sparsely populated during our visits. When I ask people to describe how they feel about work today, the first word that is volunteered is usually 'drowning'.

'This feeling matters. It's a signpost that we need to pay attention to,' says Stephenson. And many leaders agree. We initially charged forward with enthusiasm, embracing new technology, remote work and everything else the future seemed to throw at us. It worked for a while. But now, there's a palpable pullback. It's like we hit a wall, and it's not surprising. Maybe we collectively recognised that that level of effort and energy we were running at was simply unsustainable – at the same time as realising that life is, in fact, too short to work all the time. Being busy isn't as cool as it used to be. Recent data on workplace wellbeing from SuperFriend, '2023 Indicators of a Thriving Workplace', reveals a worrying trend: people across the workforce are reporting declining levels of both mental and physical health.

This is only one of several major shifts we're seeing across the workplace, and we should not underestimate how each of them will impact the way we behave, lead, innovate and develop our ability to adapt. In the context of adapting, I think there is value in briefly exploring other emerging trends that are having an impact on shaping the future of the workplace and encouraging a rethink of how we engage with change.

'Generation wellbeing'

The new rules of engagement include the clear rejection of traditional workloads by younger generations who have well-established practices around wellbeing. We only need to look at movements like the 'right to disconnect', the rise of 'anti-hustle', and the 'lying flat' trends. Each of these are explicit signals that people are no longer willing to work themselves to death.

The fact is that we're seeing younger generations across the workplace who are far more in tune with their sense of wellbeing. Younger workers grew up with a distinctly different awareness and language around taking care of themselves, and they expect the workplace to share those values. And when they discover that the 'employee value proposition' fails to live up to promises, they are comfortable opting out of a traditional job if they want to. It's in some ways refreshing to see younger people making a values-based decision without any regard for how they'll be judged. The new narrative is clear: 'I don't care if it's PwC, or KPMG – I'm not going to be a partner in exchange for burnout.'

It's also clear that we cannot respond with 'lunch and learns' that have no enduring impact. Responding with pop psychology in the workplace often oversimplifies complex issues. Wellbeing discussions in many organisations have become surface level, lacking the depth required to make meaningful changes. While it's essential to talk about mental health and wellbeing, these discussions need to be backed by expertise, not just popular trends. Otherwise, organisations risk promoting wellbeing initiatives that feel performative rather than substantive, further hindering their ability to adapt to real challenges.

This shift, fuelled by the rise of flexible workstyles and the fast-forwarding of workplace dynamics due to Covid, has empowered people to leave roles that don't meet their standards. However, this flexibility comes with its own set of challenges: business is now trying to balance employee wellbeing with the need for productivity, and it's unclear where the middle ground lies between personal care and dedication to work. This generational shift also impacts adaptability, as organisations struggle to meet evolving expectations while maintaining their own structure and goals.

Leading in an age of increased legislation

One of the issues starting to reveal itself slowly but surely is that we're creating an environment where people simply don't want to lead anymore. Many leaders, managers and small business owners in my ecosystem have scaled back, or opted not to grow their business entirely, purely based on the complicated nature of what it means today to manage people. They say it's too risky, too exhausting and fraught with concern about psychosocial legislation. Let me be clear: it's a great development that we are increasingly protected from bad behaviour at work. But legislative measures designed to protect workers, while important, have added layers of formality that impact how people view their roles. When everything is interpreted through the lens of legislation – whether it's behavioural norms or interpersonal interactions – there's less room for creative leadership and adaptability. Leaders, in particular, are under more pressure than ever, and rather than taking risks, many are retreating to familiar, 'safe' practices, which limits their ability to adapt to change.

Leadership styles have also shifted, focusing more on individual preferences rather than the needs of the team. This approach hinders adaptability because effective leadership requires adjusting to the demands of the workforce. In contrast, structured environments like the military train leaders to adopt styles that serve the group, fostering greater adaptability. Leaders are under pressure due to increased legislative frameworks but rather than adapting creatively, they are retreating to familiar, safe practices. This stifles flexibility and adaptability in leadership.

When did we start outlawing the truth about change?

'Change communication doesn't always need to be positive; it just needs to be honest,' says Stephenson. And we all know she's right. We need a new way forward regarding how we approach change in the workplace because the current methods often fail to address the reality that change is constant and messy. As Stephenson points out, the narrative around change is often overly positive, pushing for stability in times where none exists. What's truly needed is more honesty in how we communicate about change – acknowledging the discomfort and uncertainty that comes with it, rather than glossing over these realities.

Real adaptability is about balancing the protection of employees while also allowing flexibility for absorbing and negotiating change. This means accepting that disorder might be the new normal for the foreseeable future. By being more honest and relaxed about the challenges change brings, we can foster a healthier, more adaptive work environment.

'We need to be more relaxed about change. It's not easy, but it's that simple,' says Stephenson. 'We need to accept that it could be years before we bring a new sense of order to the disorder that we've experienced.'

How we typically respond to change

Before we start to explore how we can adapt more effectively to change, it's fundamental that we know how we typically behave when faced with a shift.

Deny, deny, deny

We all know someone who is flatly in denial about change. That person who refuses to upgrade the software on their device; the retail business that refuses to move to a digital platform; the family member who never does any estate planning because death is somehow not relevant to them. Denying change is a short-lived game, but one many of us play. The steep downside of denial is that the closer we get to the point of change impact, the more we forfeit control of the consequences. For instance, the business collapses and goes into liquidation; our computer crashes, costing us valuable time and money; or the federal government seizes the estate because there is no power of attorney or living will in place. In one particular case I know of, a young female friend of mine has not inherited any financials, but *has* inherited five years of administrative tasks to interpret 25 different bank accounts and a web of investments, all the while leaving the estate open to a series of insincere 'claims'. Not having your affairs in order must be one of the greatest acts of denial.

Relinquish and retreat

For some, if you say the word 'change', they only hear the word 'loss'. This can look like a person unhappy in their job who's very happy to complain relentlessly about it over an extended period of time to friends, yet refuses to take any action to find a new role. Or the person who is talking about needing to lose weight before their 50th birthday while at the same time claiming they don't have time to work out. This response is about believing change is happening *to* us, shrugging our shoulders, and making a choice to be a victim in some form. Those who relinquish and retreat often assign an immediate sense of loss to change, instead of a gain. Sometimes the loss is very real, in other cases it's not. But the gain is only realised over time. Loss can come in many forms, but primarily:

- **Loss of relationships**: Changes in personal or professional life can lead to the loss of social connections. Moving to a new place, leaving a job or even shifts in personal dynamics can cause us to lose relationships or alter the way we relate to others.
- **Loss of status**: Career changes or being made redundant can lead to a perceived or real loss of status or position, which can affect self-esteem and how others view us. This can be particularly challenging in workplace changes, when a restructure is not handled respectfully.
- **Loss of security**: Change often disrupts our sense of security, whether financial, emotional or psychological. A job change, for instance, might threaten financial stability, while personal changes can make us feel emotionally vulnerable.
- **Loss of control**: When change happens, it often feels imposed without input or consent, leading to a sense of powerlessness. Even when there's an upside to change, the loss of control can be deeply unsettling, making it hard for people to embrace. This is particularly true in

the workplace, when employees feel that key decisions affecting their work are being made without their involvement, which can cause tension between teams and their leaders.

- **Loss of pride in past achievements:** We're proud of the work we do, whether that's for a business, a community or even in our backyard. If a change is introduced, we can take that as a suggestion that our work is inferior.
- **Loss of familiarity:** We're hardwired to love routine, to thrive on autopilot. Our brains work hard to establish a pattern that is predictable, so we can cognitively kick back, conserve energy and feel safe. This sense of safety is embedded in evolutionary survival – unpredictability can be associated with threats, whereas patterns suggest stability.
- **Loss of alignment with our personal storyline:** We're attached to our story, our identity and our job – and why wouldn't we be? Many of us work hard to build a life, a social circle and a reputation on what we do best. So any sudden change to our life script feels like the plot twist we didn't see coming. Any interruption to our narrative can feel like a genuine threat to the bestselling screenplay that we've worked hard to write over many years.
- **Loss of our comfort zone:** We do love a good comfort zone, complete with exceptional coffee and snacks,

because, again, we've worked tirelessly to earn it. Take the 'work from home' policy as an example. Before March 2020, many of us were probably thinking we deserved more flexibility; we deserved to be treated like adults. So when we shifted to WFH as the norm, we felt as though we'd earned it. Now we're seeing 'back to the office' being mandated, and coming back out of our comfort zone is – let's just say for the majority – not going to happen. This is one comfort zone many are prepared to fight for.

- **Loss of time:** Change takes time. And we're already running short on it, so the idea of learning a new system, approach or procedure when we're already 'maxed out' is straight-up inconvenient. We assume that mistakes, iterations and delays are inevitable during this learning phase, which adds to the time we'll lose from being our usually productive selves.

When loss equals more gain than pain

Then we have the outliers. The 'high-AQ' thinkers.

These are people who rarely see the loss because they're focused on the gain that change brings. Commonly entrepreneurs, the outliers actively disrupt the status quo. These high-AQ outliers not only expect change, they usually create it. Completely at ease with running experiments, they trade on their ability to anticipate and influence how change happens in their world. Their attitude is that 'change happens *for* them, never *to* them'.

These are people with 'high-AQ habits', individuals with a high sense of personal agency. They have confidence in their ability to consistently act as an effective agent for themselves, to make effective decisions, and to continue to create and deliver value for a business, regardless of the circumstances. This is the entrepreneur who creates a sustainable business, instead of pursuing a change to legislation on waste reform; the commercial pilot who runs a scenario in a simulator that far exceeds the certification boundaries; the secretary who saw her boss learning to use a computer in the early 2000s, and responded by rewriting her job description to include all the things a computer could not do.

Only with distance can we usually see that in most cases a perceived loss in the moment has, in fact, led us to a gain. One of my mantras is that 'rejection is protection', and if I stare in my own personal rear-view mirror to reflect on major changes through my life so far, I can't see one that has, in the long run, not ended up showering me with gains. Being made redundant, missing out on a property, having my heart broken, being passed over for a promotion. In the moment, sure, it felt highly personal. But as time passed, the pain turned to gain.

What does high-AQ leadership look like?

As it turns out, there is compelling proof about the positives of adaptability on our leadership and lives.

An in-depth study of 1000 American business leaders published in the *Harvard Business Review* revealed that 'great leaders were defined less by enduring traits and more by their ability to recognise and adapt to opportunities created by a particular moment'. The study's author, Nitin Nohria, said, 'They could sense the zeitgeist – the spirit, mood, ideas, and beliefs that define a period – and seize it.'

In a hectic and high-pressure world where business, tech and social justice collide more frequently, we all want to make the right moves. But what does that look like? I've listed a few examples of leaders who stand out because of the courage and confidence they displayed by writing a new script to deal with an untested scenario. Let's break down some key moves.

Contextual intelligence: This is not as complicated as it sounds – basically, adaptable leaders understand what's happening around them and adjust their strategy to match. Take Tim Cook at Apple. After Steve Jobs's era of category defining products, Cook shifted Apple's focus to streamlining processes, optimising supply chains and diversifying Apple's ecosystem. He didn't try to be Jobs 2.0; he read the landscape and figured out where Apple needed to go next. That's what adaptability looks like – reading the room and leading in the moment, when others would possibly be lost, or stick to a script that the business is attached to.

Resilience: Resilient leaders work the problem until there's a collective win. Bob Chapek at Disney is an example of this. When the company initially stayed silent on Florida's controversial 'Don't Say Gay' bill, it faced backlash from both employees and customers. Chapek had to quickly adjust, publicly apologise and take a stand. His tenure may have been short-lived, but this U-turn demonstrated that resilience is a doing word. You have to practise it to build it.

Deep empathy: This is about understanding people. It's not just about making decisions; it's knowing how those decisions affect others. Ken Frazier, former CEO of Merck, gained traction for this when he led corporate America's response to the Black Lives Matter movement. He didn't just talk the talk – he took real action, driving initiatives to hire and promote more Black Americans. Leaders like Frazier know that leading with empathy builds trust and loyalty.

Innovation: Always thinking ahead, testing boundaries and finding new ways to stay ahead of the game. Whether it's in tech, finance or sustainability, these leaders understand change. They're not afraid to break from a well-established path, try something new and publicly self-correct when the stakes are high.

In short, adaptable leaders today are part strategist, part futurist, part optimist, part problem solver, and all about the people. Because it's almost impossible to promote change on any scale in isolation.

An expanded definition of adaptability

Whether you lead a small business, or a team across a large-scale organisation, you'll already know that 'leadership' is a noisy, crowded place. You only have to log into LinkedIn to be bombarded by ideas of what leadership looks like.

Undeniably, it is about many things, but in my humble view, it's mostly about knowing what you need to know *now*, and what you need to leave behind that's no longer aligned with where we find ourselves.

Leadership, in a practical sense, has undergone a radical transformation over the past few decades. The traditional model of top-down, directive leadership is not fast or flexible enough to keep up – it's being replaced by a more dynamic form that prioritises flexibility, a high tolerance for ambiguity and the courage to demonstrate creative leadership.

When I speak to business leaders and learners about adaptability, I put it in the context of IQ, EQ and AQ.

IQ is our intelligence quotient. It measures our ability to reason. It's what lands us the job.

EQ is our emotional quotient, otherwise known as emotional intelligence. It helps us understand our own feelings and those of others. It helps us get along with others.

And AQ is our adaptive quotient, or adaptive intelligence. It measures our ability to adapt to, and lead through, change and uncertainty. AQ gives us staying power. It's a portal to high performance and feeling confident about co-creating a future that we want to be part of.

High-AQ leaders are exceptional at connecting dots; they're flexible thinkers, they're obsessed with learning, they know that resilience is a 'doing' word, and they are fully engaged with the signals of change. As I mentioned in the Introduction, pilots are in constant conversation with change. They train for it; they plan for it. They understand that what is true now might not be true in a few minutes. They acknowledge that anything is possible. They obsess over it, because the cost of failure in aviation is so great.

So if the job of a leader is to act as a watchtower of sorts, surely it makes sense to consider the question: what if we behaved more like pilots when it comes to adapting to change?

I posed this question in September 2024 to Captain Richard de Crespigny, who was the pilot-in-command of QF32, the A380 that suffered an uncontained engine failure shortly after taking off from Singapore's Changi Airport on 4 November 2010. Despite multiple system failures and severe damage to an engine, the veteran aviator managed to return to Changi Airport and land the Airbus safely. Captain de Crespigny has been widely praised for his exceptional leadership, both in the cockpit and after the plane landed, when he insisted on addressing passengers in detail, then handed out his mobile number so anyone could call if they had questions or needed help – a truly remarkable move.

Captain de Crespigny tells me: 'Adaptability is everything. When the winds of change blow, some people build walls, others build windmills. Those who build walls become laggards, targets, dinosaurs and irrelevant. In contrast, those who build windmills embrace and harness change. They adapt and align with disruption, unlocking limitless opportunities. To ensure our survival and success, we must commit to a lifetime of learning, adaption and embracing change.'

Adaptive intelligence: from responding to pre-empting

In this context, adaptability is not just about responding to change; it's about pre-empting change and leading it. We must be able to identify what's changing around us, be open-minded about new ideas, and be willing to question well-established, long-held beliefs that may no longer be fit for purpose. This requires a learner who is willing to step into the fundamentals of futures thinking. While both fields are concerned with dealing with change, *adapting* focuses on maintaining stability, effectiveness and alignment in the process of change in the present or near future. *Futures thinking*, on the other hand, is about anticipating and preparing for various possible futures, and practising foresight to move towards a preferred future, instead of one that is projected or plausible. Both are crucial for navigating an increasingly uncertain world, but they operate at different time scales and with different goals. We need a combination of both – we need to expand our traditional definition of adaptability to meet a new era.

These are some of the key fundamentals that provide some context for where we are now, and where to go next; the current state of play across the workplace, how we typically respond to change and the proven role of adaptability in defining effective leadership. There is one more fundamental I'd like to reflect on before we talk about the four ways to master change – and that's how we define success. Because when we're clear on what success looks like to us, we become anchored in what matters most and we have a foundation for making decisions that are intentional.

2

Modern success metrics

*Think back ten years.
What did you believe to be true
that is no longer true?*

When Morgan Coleman was contacted by the *New York Times* for an interview in 2019, he thought it was a joke. Despite racking up an impressive list of accolades and achieving media coverage for his fast-growing start-up, Vets On Call – dubbed 'Uber for vets' – the 28-year-old entrepreneur still couldn't quite believe that one of the world's prestigious and most-read newspapers wanted to talk to him.

As he told me in a 2024 interview, Coleman was achieving much of the success he'd dreamed of – publicity, status and role-modelling for his Indigenous peers. As a proud Torres Strait Islander Indigenous Australian, Coleman grew up in regional Victoria and remembers the lack of visible Indigenous role models outside of sport. He felt like his pathways were limited, linear and predictable.

A residential scholarship to the University of Melbourne's Trinity College provided a path to academic achievement but also opened his eyes to the possibilities available to him. Being among 'people who wanted more for themselves' – sons and daughters of Australia's business leaders and politicians – was life-changing for Coleman. 'Everyone believed they could create an amazing life for themselves, so I started believing it too.' His definition of success was evolving by the day; he wanted more for himself, and he wanted to become the role model that he had lacked growing up.

This belief had served him well early in his career, giving him the courage to turn his back on a successful corporate career with a multinational development and construction company to embark on his entrepreneurial journey.

In less than four years, he built Vets on Call to AU$1 million annual revenue, with 12,000 customers and 80 vets working across three cities, but desperately needed venture capital to scale the business.

When the *New York Times* article was published, reality did not entirely match his expectations. He thought he'd wake up to thousands of new followers and contacts, but he only got 30 – and none led to new business or funding opportunities. Despite the publicity he was attracting and the hours he was putting in, it wasn't translating to business success or the financial abundance he was trying to build. It was the beginning of his shift away from correlating visibility and status with success, and towards focusing more on what really mattered to him.

Coleman recalls a pivotal moment in his life when his practice of looking inward really began. Waking up anxious on the eve of his 30th birthday, with his wife pregnant with their first child, he felt a crushing sense of failure that he was almost 30 and still not a millionaire – this was the ambitious target he'd set for himself in the halls at Trinity College. There's more to the story, but he ended up exiting Vets on Call in 2022 to focus on other ventures, including helping to establish the first Indigenous angel investment platform, Blak Angels.

For Coleman, success now equals freedom, and other people's opinions of whether or not he meets their definition of success have been sidelined.

He's focused on having freedom in his time, location and pursuit of opportunities, with family and health at the top of his priorities, and personal growth right up there too. His version of success is still very dependent on maintaining a level of financial security, but he's acutely aware that money doesn't directly give him the things he values most; it's simply an enabler. His filter for anything that's going to require his time has more checkpoints now; time spent away from his two kids must directly align with his definition of personal success.

Coleman credits his business journey for the lessons in connecting to what he really wants and teaching him the true meaning of success. Today, he is extremely reflective and shows a lot of self-insight. He is deeply intentional about how he uses his time and actively reviews his goals weekly. He says he reverse-engineers results from where he wants to be, focusing on the actions he needs to take now to achieve his goals.

The result of this intention and relentless pursuit of what's truly important according to his latest definition of success? He feels far more successful than the folder of *New York Times*, *Forbes* and other press clippings ever made him feel.

Who defined success anyway?

Coleman's story is an interesting case study of the success myths that most of us live by: definitions of success handed to us by society, our families, schools, friends, partners and community. Or, simply, the 'shoulds' we've accepted for ourselves without much interrogation. Many of us fail to realise that we're living within an invisible, made-up construct of what it means to be successful; we're mentally trapped in an outdated way of defining success. Before we look at how to be a proactive player in our own transformation, we need to be clear on what success means to us, so we can stay anchored in our truth – and not someone else's.

A short history of success

In his 1989 global bestseller, *The 7 Habits of Highly Effective People*, author Stephen Covey details how he reviewed over 200 years of literature on success published in the United States. Covey was drawn to the topic because, after 25 years of working with people in business, university and family settings, he noted that he'd met many people who had achieved incredible outward success, but found themselves struggling with a yearning for personal connection, a sense of belonging and deep relationships with other people.

Covey's interrogation of the success literature published in the US since 1976 included reviewing hundreds of books, articles and essays on things like self-improvement, philosophy and popular psychology, and revealed an interesting distinction in the way that success was defined.

The first 150 or so years of writing focused on what Covey called the 'Character Ethic' as the foundation of success – things like integrity, humility, fidelity, temperance, courage, justice, patience, simplicity and modesty. In other words, traits commonly synonymous with 'fulfilment'. He wrote that the Character Ethic was made up of several fundamentals that comprise a good life. When people prioritise these principles in their lives, they can experience long-term happiness and meaningful success.

But in the wake of World War I, there was a shift in the basic understanding of success. Covey noted that during this time, success started to be defined more as a function of personality, relating to public image, attitudes and behaviours, skills and techniques that act as a primer for human interaction. In other words, more outward-facing, perceptible traits rather than a deep inner sense of fulfilment. Around this time was also when the 'positive mental attitude' or PMA thinking was popularised.

This shift signalled a change from evaluating success from a place of inner knowing to an outward projection. It was like shifting from seeing through to your soul in a mirror, looking deep into your own eyes and feeling contentment, to looking only at the image reflected back to you, dressing it appropriately depending on the latest fashion or trend, and heading out to seek external validation for your choices – a metaphor for the likes-and-shares-obsessed world of social media that, for so many, has become a proxy for evaluating success.

One of the most powerful actions we can take is to redefine success to provide ourselves with a compass point. Success as fulfilment is a good place to start. We'll explore this more later in the chapter, but for now it's helpful to identify some of the success myths that have been unconsciously running the show for many of us.

The multiple success myths

We live in a world obsessed with a specific definition of success: the high-status job, the conventional rise through the corporate ranks and the mostly fake prestige attached to starting up and scaling up a business. We've been railroaded into living by multiple success myths.

Many of us crafted our success metrics, either consciously or unconsciously, in the context of a different time. A time when completing school, getting a degree and working in a 'safe' job for a 'good' company was a fail-safe path to economic stability, peace and choice.

Many of us have adopted these myths without evaluating whether they're fit for purpose or aligned with our values. These traditional versions of success focus on outdated models, but somewhat ironically are often amplified by the modern overlay of social media.

Let's recap some of these myths.

The money myth

The myth that money will fix all our problems, make us happy and signal our success to the world. In reality, in the words of Dave Ramsey, we are buying things we don't need with money we don't have to impress people we don't like. There's no question that money plays an important role in modern society, and financial security is going to underpin most versions of success. But the myth that it will make all our problems go away is quickly dispelled by looking around.

The status myth

This can come in so many forms, and it's amplified by social media. If we don't post it, did it really happen? While it's true that people's perception of us is influenced by what they see online, Coleman's story is a telling example of how status and publicity does not necessarily lead to the outcomes we think it might.

The productivity and achievement myths

Again, social media is great at feeding the productivity and achievement myths. It's hard not to feel like you're underperforming if you're simply holding down a job, looking after yourself and being a good person. Where's the side hustle? The self-improvement? The post with the number of books you read last month? After all, we all end up in the same place – and most people's 'achievements' will be summed up in less than 30 minutes.

The happy family myth

Like the money myth, this is one of the enduring stories we tell ourselves and each other, through our thirties in particular: everything will be better if I have a loving partner and children. If you're single in your forties – or partnered but choose not to have children – it almost always, in quiet ways, stirs questions and determines your suitability for certain circles, circles that prefer not to include people whose choices differ from theirs.

There are many more myths like this: the unicorn start-up myth; the promotion myth; the happiness myth; the travel-for-work myth; the sea-change myth – the list goes on.

Whose version of success are you following?

If your identity is closely linked to or depends on your work status, job or ability to provide, then there are few life events more destabilising than having the career rug pulled unexpectedly from underneath you – or indeed any major career change that feels like a departure from the script you have for yourself.

When I turned my back on my decade-long television reporting career in 2012 – a career that had taken me across the world, into war zones, onto Capitol Hill and into conversation with some of the world's most interesting people – the sense of destabilisation was overwhelming. I loved my time in media. Throughout my news career, I never missed a deadline and genuinely got along with just about everyone. When I was forced out of my job due to relentless workplace bullying and culture problems, I was an emotional trainwreck. I was also flat broke, with few work prospects; I borrowed grocery money from my friends for an entire year. I told my bank that I could not pay my mortgage until further notice. My tax return tells me I made AU$25,000 that year, which feels about right.

The comeback was slow and humiliating. I had to lean deeply into what my success metrics were, to identify my signposts and hike my way back to 'success'.

The truth is, we can always make a change, but it often requires us to redefine success and have the courage to step into the world that aligns with our new definition.

This was brought sharply into focus as I embarked on my entrepreneur journey and set up my business, initially focused on media training for corporate executives in Australia and later running global leadership programs for top talent across some of the world's best companies. If I had entertained my success myths – other people's versions of what success looked like for me – I wouldn't have achieved any of what I have over the past decade. Their version of success for me was seeing me on the evening news. 'Just approach another network, or go overseas again!' was a phrase I heard daily. But I saw a new vision. My new definition of success wasn't tied to a television newsroom.

The new success metrics

If we're going to talk about how we negotiate change with a view to where we're headed, then it makes sense to start by examining what success looks like for us.

The paradigm shift in values, behaviours and attitudes towards work, purpose and meaning hit us hard in 2020, and the years since. Everything we know is now subject to change without notice: we learnt that governments can literally shut down the world, stop offices from operating and impact businesses in ways we couldn't have imagined before. Many of us learnt some hard truths during the pandemic: work matters, but it's not everything. And those who navigated home schooling multiple children alongside maintaining some level of productivity also learnt that they can withstand more pressure than they'd previously imagined.

About three-quarters of the people I speak to enjoyed the change in pace brought on by the pandemic, the simplification and focus on the small things that remained within our control. The lack of expectation around holidays, interstate family obligations, extracurricular activities. Yet for others, the pace change was a brutal reminder of how important social activity is to their wellbeing.

More frequently, we're seeing people opt out of a predictable path of climbing the traditional ladder of success to pursue their own version of a favoured future, a preferred future that brings a deeper sense of meaning and personal fulfilment. I see people I admire slowly defining success in entirely new terms, prioritising:

- time and balance (to spend with friends, family, doing hobbies, etc.)
- creative freedom
- health
- a stronger sense of wellbeing
- connections and community.

Success at its core is deeply personal. One of the greatest gifts to come out of the pandemic was the opportunity to look more closely at how we're designing our lives; to get off the treadmill, focus on our success myths and look at how we can replace traditional definitions of success with new metrics that are aligned with our values.

I believe that for the first time in the modern history of work, this is the opportunity available to many of us – a wide-open window to reconsider our individual success metrics and find *even small ways* to let go of what may no longer be 'fit for purpose'. In this extraordinary new chapter, we have the opportunity – *but not necessarily the skills* – to imagine, influence and plan a more rewarding path.

So where do we start with rethinking our personal success metrics – and moving forward to find a slightly more fulfilling future?

It starts with being clear on what's important to us and our future.

Sometimes we need to look back to look forward

Reanna Browne, an academically trained and practising futurist, says in a 2024 personal interview that the starting point for any futures work always lies in the past.

She posits that *good futurists are good historians*, citing several reasons:

- We look back to illuminate bigger stories of change over time and to consider what this might mean for us in the future.
- We look back to question and expand our understanding of what's possible in our futures.

Looking back to assess and understand how much change we are capable of, specifically around what 'success' means to us, is a powerful exercise. This is the starting point for understanding change and what we need to be paying attention to. How have *we* changed in the past five, ten, fifteen years?

Browne says: 'The present, with all its clarity, can also box us in, limiting our vision for what is possible tomorrow. But our history, rich with insights and precedents, can sometimes unearth a robust foundation to broaden our imagination of what's possible. Take women's sports, for instance. Most of us think large audiences for women's sport are a recent trend, a sign of our progressive times. Yet a look back reveals a different story. In 1929, a women's Australian rules football match at the Adelaide Oval drew 41,000 fans, challenging the notion that our enthusiasm for women's sports is new. Using the past as a powerful tool, we can build agency and expand our range of "thinkable futures" in the present.'

Small moves that change a long game

Making a small move in a long game is a low-risk, low-cost experiment to test before we invest. It's a way to explore new possibilities in a safe way. Each small move provides valuable feedback, helping us uncover what's emerging without requiring a precise 'big' end goal. Instead of fixating on a specific outcome, these incremental actions keep us engaged with changing circumstances, revealing new pathways as we move forward. Change doesn't always have to be attached to one big and bold ambition. Meaningful change often begins with modest, adjacent steps. For instance, consider someone contemplating a career change but uncertain about their next move. Instead of diving into an all-or-nothing decision, they could begin with exploratory actions: showing up to an industry event, connecting with professionals in the field, or taking a skill-building course. Over time, these incremental actions build momentum, driving a meaningful shift and demonstrating that real change starts with small, simple moves.

Where we water seeds, plants grow

As I write this, I'm about half a year out from turning 50 and questioning whether to celebrate with a big bash. I love birthdays and see the privilege of celebrating them as just that: a privilege. But my conversations on the topic have been instructive.

So many beautiful, high-achieving people shy away from acknowledging their 50th birthday (or indeed other milestones) because, as they share with me in private, 'I'm not where I thought I'd be.'

Wow. Yes, but are any of us?

Maybe we haven't sold a unicorn start-up (yet), landed the dream partner (yet), or gotten as fit as we'd like to be (yet). But isn't that the privilege of being where we are? Regardless of what our success metrics are, we can actually go after them and move towards a greater sense of fulfilment? Let's not lose perspective on how far we've come in life and the ark we've already built to negotiate the highest of tides.

If our habits are the silent architects of our lives, and we can define success as a deep, underlying sense of fulfilment, then it makes sense to focus our pursuit of success on who we want to be in the small moments.

It's easy to focus on the big moments – the work milestones, the public speaking opportunities, the sports competitions – and mistakenly believe that these are the times that we need to show up at our best in order to be 'successful'.

But in the same way that small moves can have a big pay-off in a long game, it's far more impactful to put more emphasis on how we show up in the everyday experiences that matter to us: time with loved ones, the conversations we have with ourselves, the value of our word (and how we honour it), the small decisions we make that edge us towards greater fulfilment. Who we are for ourselves and how that aligns with our vision. How we act and honour our word, even when no one is watching – because true success can only come from within us.

And this is where the concept of small wins comes in – because small wins compound into big wins. If we can end each day knowing we did one or two small things that align with our vision of success (if we're defining it as fulfilment), then those small habits that influence our lives will compound into meaningful returns aligned with the way we want to live.

Those small wins might be fifteen minutes of true presence with your partner; going for a walk; being conscious of where your money went and making empowered decisions around how you spend it; deleting or restricting a shopping app, social media app or anything else that's mining your time; honouring your word, even when no one else knows.

Psychologist Nicole LePera, known as 'the Holistic Psychologist', has become a global sensation courtesy of her sage advice in her 2023 book, *How to Be the Love You Seek,* and social channels. She believes that one of the most transformative and empowering things we can do for ourselves is to keep small promises to ourselves. Like small moves in a long game, what are the small things we can do to keep us on track, or stay true to what's important?

Keeping small promises to myself has been a game changer for me, because I can have all the intention in the world to switch off from social media, stop at one chocolate biscuit, or get up earlier, but the power is in the action, not just the promise.

Ash Barty: a deep connection to what really matters, on her terms

Australian professional tennis player and three-time Grand Slam winner Ash Barty surprised the world when she retired from the sport in 2022, at age 25. She was ranked number one in the world, and just two months earlier had won the Australian Open. She was at the top of her game, and arguably had at least another five years of a successful tennis career ahead of her.

But following her Australian Open win, success took on a new definition for Barty. She announced her retirement during an informal interview with her former doubles partner and close friend Casey Dellacqua, which was posted to her Instagram page. The announcement itself was an expression of her trademark simplicity, completely aligned with her values and character.

In the video, Barty acknowledged she no longer had the drive to play at an elite level, and that it was time to chase other dreams.

Noting how hard it was to say the words out loud, she also said she no longer felt compelled to do what she knows is required to be the best she can be at tennis.

Everyone loves a champion, and so many of us would have loved to have seen Barty play on, win more Grand Slams and wear the green and gold. But Barty knew it was time, and showed the world that she valued life on her terms more than a life that ticked other people's success boxes.

Barty's decision beautifully illustrates the power of personal agency: recognising how and why our goals, feelings and desires are evolving in real time, and seeing these signals of change early enough to make empowered decisions about our future.

So many of us hang on to what we've become accustomed to because we don't actively look out for these signals within ourselves. Looking out for these signals is a practice that takes courage, because it requires us to look back and evaluate what's working and what's not, and acknowledge that our priorities aren't necessarily what we thought they would be.

Barty's long-time coach, Craig Tyzzer, said in a 2019 interview on Channel 9 that Barty is 'a much better person than she is a tennis player. For me, that's been the key. A lot of people talk about her talent and her tennis, but talent only gets you so far. It's really her character that has taken her to where she is right now.'

That lauded character, and grounding in values, laid the foundation for her successful transition out of the sport.

What does all this have to do with change?

Our ability to navigate change from an empowered position is closely correlated with our adaptability quotient or AQ. As I mentioned in the Introduction, I believe upgrading your AQ is the single greatest investment you can make in your future.

Most people I know are so busy keeping their heads above water managing their career, health, family, finances, 24-hour news cycle and social media, disruptive technologies and social expectations – not to mention the macro-factors like wars, economic and political uncertainty, climate change and the latest diseases threatening another pandemic – that taking time to pause and think deeply about success is certainly not front of mind.

Even if we do make the time, knowing what it is that truly drives us can be just as difficult. Psychologist and executive coach Susan David, who authored the 2016 book, *Emotional Agility*, talks about how our emotions can help guide us towards what is truly meaningful for us: sensations like fear, anxiety, joy and exhilaration, the body's immediate physical responses to important signals from the outside world. She describes emotional agility as loosening up, calming down and living with more intention, and highlights in her book that being flexible with your thoughts and feelings is key to wellbeing and success.

As someone who is obsessed with helping people anticipate and embrace change, I couldn't agree more. As we zero in on what's truly meaningful to us and start curating our life accordingly, we free ourselves up to make better decisions, because we're basing them on our feelings and desires.

David asserts that emotionally agile people are dynamic and able to demonstrate flexibility in dealing with our fast-changing, complex world. 'They are able to tolerate high levels of stress and to endure setbacks,' she writes in *Emotional Agility*, 'while remaining engaged, open and receptive. They understand that life isn't always easy, but they continue to act according to their most cherished values and pursue their big, long-term goals.'

As we've explored throughout this chapter, our relationship to change and how well we can adapt to the avalanche of the new involves being crystal clear on what's important to us.

This clarity is what helps ground us in phases of uncertainty; it provides the compass for decision making and path-paving – which we're all having to do much more frequently, and at an accelerated pace. Understanding what gives us purpose, and what is no longer fit for purpose, is the precursor to making change work *for* us.

What does success look like for you, today?

Answering this question honestly requires us to get real with ourselves.

Are we living a life that is aligned with our values?

How are we anchoring ourselves in a life that brings us meaning and happiness?

In their 2014 article for the *Harvard Business Review*, 'What does success mean to you?', authors Professor Boris Groysberg and Robin Abrahams introduced the concept of objective and subjective success, and advised readers to evaluate their success by plotting their own success metrics in a table like the one below.

SUCCESS METRICS

	CAREER	**PERSONAL** hbr.org
Objective	Salary Job title Prestigious firm Awards and accolades	Personal achievements (e.g. running a marathon) Community involvement (e.g. teaching Sunday school) Presence at kids' events Retirement savings
Subjective	Enjoyment of work Pride in accomplishments Connection with colleagues Meaningful company mission	Happy marriage Well-adjusted children Fulfilling relationships Ability to relax and recharge

SOURCE: BORIS GROYSBERG AND ROBIN ABRAHAMS

The writers observed that a significant number of people are unaware of where they are directing their focus until they engage in an activity like this.

Drawing on research that involved almost 4000 interviews and more than 80 surveys with senior business executives asking what success meant to them in work and life, they observed that subjective factors such as 'making a difference' and 'working with a good team in a good environment' came up frequently in leaders' definitions of career success, and rewarding relationships were by far the most common element of personal success.

I undertook a similar research assignment, albeit with a far smaller sample size. In conversations with 40 people that work in the knowledge sector in Australia, Asia, Europe and the US, most people highlighted the importance of various but similar subjective factors like contributing to the greater good, prioritising quality time with family, and continuous learning in their chosen field or passion. And yet their actions and lifestyles suggested an emphasis on the objective metrics like job title, salary and the social status of their kids' schools.

I don't make this point to pass judgement or suggest it's not worth focusing on these metrics – for many of us, the objective metrics are extremely important and allow us to realise our subjective metrics. But it's crucial to be aware of how and where we're placing our energy, and to be clear on whose version of success we're living in alignment with: ours, or the one society chose for us?

Many of the corporate executives I spoke with were highly focused on objective measures of success in their jobs, which allowed them to realise more subjective measures outside work. They felt satisfied and in alignment. I think there is value in reflecting on how our traditional definitions of success metrics have changed over the last ten years and how those metrics are conveyed across social media. There are, of course, many more ways to measure success – which is entirely the point of this chapter. We all need to define what metrics matter to us.

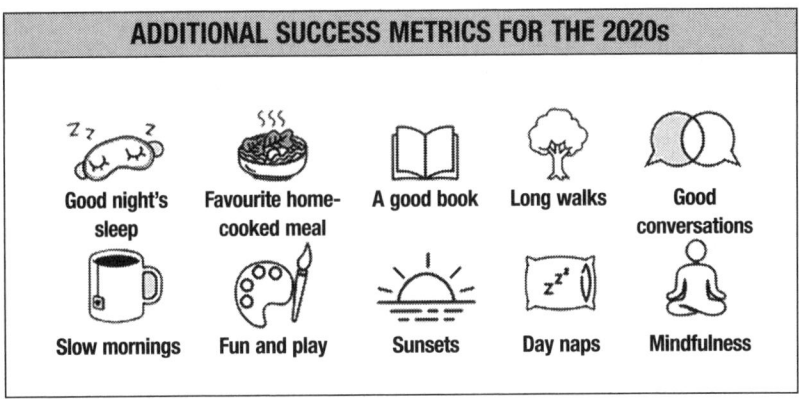

SOURCE: ANDREA CLARKE

Surprisingly, I also spoke with people who'd made tree changes during the pandemic lockdowns, escaping the office for the digital nomad life, but had ultimately decided the grass actually wasn't greener for them. I was one of those people – I moved to Kirra Beach in Queensland in June 2021. By February 2023, I had done a complete U-turn back to Sydney. While I felt in alignment for a while, the novelty wore off and I ultimately discovered that one of my fundamental success metrics was feeling a sense of belonging and community, which I essentially gave up to live in a quieter place.

Through that experience I was reminded that our success metrics are deeply personal, and they change over time in unexpected ways.

Part 2

The four principles

Engage with the signals of change.

Accept what's changing.

Activate your optimism for the new.

Release what's holding you back.

3

Engage

The first step of being in a continual conversation with change

'Look not back in anger, nor forward in fear, but around in awareness.'

James Thurber

As the sun dipped below the horizon on 14 April 1912, the wireless radio began to crackle with increased urgency. The frigid air of the North Atlantic was two degrees as ships sent desperate messages to one another, warning of treacherous icebergs lurking in the dark waters. Amid this chaos, Jack Phillips toiled away at the wireless radio aboard the RMS *Titanic*. He received a message from another ship pinpointing the location of a dense icepack and numerous bergs.

Forty minutes before the *Titanic* collided with the iceberg on 14 April, a nearby ship, the SS *Californian*, sent a distress signal, announcing that they were stranded in a field of ice. Instead of taking action, the *Titanic*'s wireless operator brushed off the warning.

'I'm busy,' he said.

Phillips was too busy to run it up the flagpole because he was preoccupied with sending and receiving personal messages for the wealthy and elite passengers on board. We all know what happened next. And though we now know the numerous factors that contributed to this tragedy, the story of what happened in the wireless room that night remains a lesser-known tale. But just imagine if the captain and crew had truly listened to the early warnings that were coming in loud and clear; if they had taken the time to truly understand the gravity of the situation. Perhaps, just perhaps, the outcome could have been different.

Change is happening all the time; we're just not taking any notice

There is, of course, more to the story about this young man's careless comment in the hours leading up to the *Titanic* sinking. Jack Phillips was a dedicated young man who was working tirelessly next to his fellow operator, Harold McBride. The *Titanic* had a revolutionary new Marconi wireless radio system installed, which actually stopped transmitting at 7 pm on 13 April. These two men defied procedure (which required them to wait until the ship docked in port and allow a certified Marconi engineer to address the failure) and worked through the night to get the radio working at around 4 am on 14 April. Phillips was running on barely any sleep once he was back on shift, where he was relentlessly playing catch-up, sending official documents and personal messages from passengers to loved ones back home which were meant to have been transmitted the night before.

There's always context. And in the moment, their actions might have felt logical and warranted. They were playing a high-pressure game of catch-up on a remarkable public maiden voyage while running on barely any sleep. Both operators were on an 'unsinkable' ship, so there must have been an extreme element of unconscious bias embedded into their mindset when it came to being warned about icebergs. This is a history lesson that is so profoundly relevant for both leaders and teams in modern times: if we ignore a signal of change in our world, regardless of how justified we believe we are in ignoring it, it remains a signal that has the potential to intensify over time, and inevitably impact us. And usually, the longer we leave it, the more damage it can do. (For example, if you were running a bricks-and-mortar retail store and ignored intensifying signals about having an online presence, by the time you decide to activate an e-commerce store, you find yourself competing with faster, cheaper competitors).

When we dig into the backstory of exactly how the *Titanic* sank, the story gets worse, and the lesson is reinforced. And it becomes a powerful exercise in the cost of having a fixed mindset – a mindset that opts to dismiss warning signs in order to 'stay the course'. You see, it was not one ship calling in to report one iceberg. The RMS *Titanic* received a total of seven iceberg warnings on the day it struck the iceberg, 14 April 1912. These warnings came from various ships in the vicinity, reporting large ice fields and iceberg sightings in the North Atlantic.

1. 9 am – from the RMS *Caronia*, warning of 'bergs, growlers, and field ice'.
2. 1.42 pm – from the RMS *Baltic*, reporting large quantities of ice.
3. 1.45 pm – from the SS *Amerika*, sent to the US Hydrographic Office but relayed to the *Titanic*, about two large icebergs.
4. 7.30 pm – from the SS *Californian*, warning of three large icebergs.
5. 7.50 pm – From the SS *Mesaba*, reporting heavy pack ice and a large number of icebergs.
6. 9.40 pm – from the SS *Californian*, reporting a field of ice directly in the *Titanic*'s path.
7. 10.30 pm – another warning from the SS *Californian*, which was not delivered to the bridge. The SS *Californian* had stopped for the night due to heavy ice.

Despite these seven reports, the *Titanic* continued to travel at almost full speed, striking an iceberg at 11.40 pm.

Look up and out at what is changing

As if the sinking of the *Titanic* isn't tragic enough, it's even more so when we scan this list of warnings and realise it could have been avoided on multiple occasions throughout the day. This is a shocking and powerful example of why we need to 'look up and out' at what is happening around us. If we're too busy to look up and out, we don't give ourselves any chance to adapt to the change that's coming for us; we have no braking distance between ourselves and the point of impact. There is less time to change course and fewer options available to us, so we forfeit the opportunity to control the outcome. If we deny, dismiss or disregard a signal, we only delay the impact it's likely to have.

This is a key part of *Adapt*: the earlier we are truly engaged with change, the more time we give ourselves to prepare for change and shape the way it lands around us.

Principle #1: Engage

Be an active player in change by engaging with and understanding how it happens. Actively recognise, interpret and respond to early indicators that suggest a shift in trends, behaviours or environments. Consider how you can deliberately create space to engage with incremental change factors that will impact your life.

High-AQ habits that support this principle:
- scan for signals of change
- obsess over learning
- propagate a 3D network.

High-AQ habit: Scan for signals of change
How change happens

Change can happen fast, and change can also happen slowly. But regardless of the speed, direction or scale, it always has one common thread: it interrupts familiar patterns and routines, creating space for something new to emerge.

There are three factors that shape change: drivers, signals and patterns. Think of them as being like weather patterns that lead to a storm.

Drivers are like the large, invisible forces that create the conditions for a storm – think of the wind currents, air pressure or ocean temperatures. You can't always see these forces directly, but they're powerful and constantly working in the background, shaping what's to come. For example, the rise of digital technology or shifting social values are the 'climate' changes that push us toward new ways of thinking and operating.

Signals are like the dark clouds rolling in, or the first raindrops. They're the early warning signs that something's about to happen. They might seem small or scattered at first, but if you pay attention, they tell you a bigger storm is brewing. These could be new customer behaviours, emerging technologies, or a sudden buzz around a fresh idea – clues that change is on the way.

Trends are the full-blown storm. They're the recognisable patterns that everyone can see, like the heavy rain or strong winds that confirm the storm is here. When you notice a trend, it means those early signals have gathered enough momentum to reshape the landscape, whether it's a shift in workplace culture or a new industry standard. So, just like watching the sky, if you can spot the drivers, pick up on the signals and understand the trends, you can get ahead of the storm – or better yet, use it to your advantage.

Paying attention to signals of change

There are many ways to engage with the change happening around us, and, when we think about cultivating high-AQ habits, paying attention to the signals is a natural place to start. Change often begins as a small signal – subtle shifts that grow into larger waves of transformation. When we are consistently scanning for signals, we're becoming our own futurist, through the practice of recognising patterns that may lead to broader trends or disruptions that we can be active players in.

A signal of change is a left-field, surprising example of a small, local change that disrupts the everyday established order, or the status quo. A signal points to how the future could be different to today. Change is happening all the time; we're just not necessarily taking notice. Like a modern-day version of Jack Phillips triaging the calls, notifications and daily demands placed upon us, we're just 'too busy' to look up from our phones to acknowledge even the weakest signals of change: we might have driven past the young schoolgirl holding a sign outside a Swedish parliament in 2018 that read 'School Strike for Climate', or disinterestedly scanned a news article about the young tech CEO who declared his staff could 'work from anywhere' in May 2020.

These two particular events met the two criteria for a signal of change:
1. **Potentially surprising:** It's 'out of left field'.
2. **Specific:** It clearly and directly relates to a particular change, helping to separate meaningful patterns from general noise.

Signal superpower

Having a regular scanning practice can be a low-effort, high-reward power move, whether you're an individual or a business. When we recognise signals early enough, they can act as an early warning system, providing valuable time to anticipate and prepare for future changes. This proactive stance helps manage potential risks and allows us to seize new opportunities months and sometimes years before they turn into a mainstream trend. I have a personal case study to share here about the power of recognising a signal in your own life – and not dismissing it.

A personal signal of change

In early 2008, the news industry was about to experience a seismic shift, and I found myself standing in the middle of it – quite literally – on K Street in Washington, DC, heading to the Al Jazeera English news bureau. As I passed a newsstand, something happened that brought me to an unconscious halt. I slowed down and stopped in the middle of the footpath, oblivious to everyone moving around me. It was a moment of profound realisation, playing out in slow motion.

For years, I had a well-established habit of picking up a newspaper on my way to work. It was as routine as brushing my teeth. But on this particular morning, something was different. Instead of buying a copy of the *New York Times*, I instinctively glanced at my phone for the headlines.

Today, this wouldn't seem like a big deal. Why would it, when we check our phones 96 times a day on average, and scanning the news has become part of those checks? But here was the distinction: my behaviour towards consuming news had just changed. I was a journalist, paid to produce news that I was no longer willing to pay for as a consumer. In that instant, I realised: I was the signal. And what if my behaviour scaled? What if tens of thousands of people just like me stopped buying newspapers and switched to their phones for news? As I walked those 100 steps to the newsroom, the glass doors in the distance, I knew: the business model of news was collapsing around me.

Within those steps, I started running scenarios in my head, and none of them felt good. Social media was brutally disrupting traditional news, fracturing audiences, and upending a habit ingrained in millions of households – tuning in to the 6 pm news was now optional. I was already working twelve-hour shifts, six days a week. I knew I was on a collision course with burnout, and I couldn't work any harder or faster. Any downward pressure on the newsroom business model would eventually land on my desk – longer shifts, less pay, fewer viewers. Worse still, the longer I stayed, the more time I forfeited to learn new skills. Business often talks about 'cash burn', but what I saw was 'career burn'.

By the time I swiped into the newsroom on the fourth floor, I had decided: I was leaving journalism. There were other warning signs, but this one was flashing the brightest, the one I couldn't ignore.

The decision was going to be disruptive, yes. But not nearly as disruptive as it would have been had I left it in limbo for a decade. That morning's micro-signal – the moment I reached for my phone instead of the *New York Times* – was the catalyst for reimagining my career and getting ahead of the profound shift that played out over the following years. It met the criteria for a signal of change: it was a specific example of what was changing, and it surprised me. And if the signal scaled, although it might take five to ten years, it would definitely affect my future.

This moment wasn't just a lesson in recognising signals of change – it was a call to action. Taking pre-emptive action gave me options. The longer I stayed in journalism, the more I would over-index on one set of skills. Leaving television in 2008 meant I could explore new industries, build new skills and ultimately stay more employable, giving me a few years before I ran into my colleagues at the same job interview.

I share this with you because sometimes the clearest signal of change is in the mirror. Pay attention to yourself and your behaviour – it may be sending you the signal you need.

From personal to business: signals that shape entire industries

Just as individuals can recognise personal signals of change, businesses face their own critical moments. The ability to identify and act on these signals often determines whether they will own the market or become obsolete. Take Netflix, for example – a company that not only paid attention to the shifting landscape but also made bold, pre-emptive moves in response. I know that the Netflix case study is a very common example of adapting, but not enough people have a true appreciation for just how well the leadership team at Netflix have played all of the signals, one after the other. It's not only about identifying what's changing – it's having the confidence and courage to make effective decisions to pre-empt the opportunity a signal presents.

Many of you will know the background. In the late 1990s and early 2000s, Netflix was primarily a DVD rental-by-mail service. I was living in Washington, DC, at the time and remember the transition vividly, because I had to wait 45 minutes to download a movie.

And here is where things started to get interesting. By the mid-2000s, the leadership at Netflix began noticing a few key signals that indicated the future of media consumption was likely to shift towards streaming.

Settling into the background as a significant driver of change was the growing adoption of high-speed internet, which made online video streaming more feasible.

Running parallel to this was the first signal – content licensing shifts. Netflix noticed that studios and networks were increasingly willing to license their content to digital platforms, creating a window of opportunity for streaming services. This shift indicated that traditional content owners were recognising digital distribution as a viable revenue source, even if they were hesitant to develop streaming models themselves. This shift in content licensing not only signalled a change in how media companies valued digital platforms but also gave Netflix the opportunity to expand its library, making streaming more appealing to consumers.

The second signal was changing consumer behaviour. There was a gradual but clear shift in the way consumers wanted to access content – we wanted it faster, and when it suited us. And the third signal was the decline of physical media: sales of physical DVDs began to slow, indicating a potential decline in demand for DVD rentals. Netflix connected the signals and saw a pattern of change emerging. The company started experimenting with video streaming as early as 2007, even though its core business was still DVD rentals. It invested in building the technology needed to support streaming while simultaneously expanding its content library. By the time streaming became mainstream in the early 2010s, Netflix was already a market leader, well ahead of traditional media companies and other competitors. This early pivot not only saved the company from potential obsolescence but also allowed it to grow into a global entertainment powerhouse.

Signals help us identify risk
But this was just the first of three masterful moves by the co-founder of Netflix, Reed Hastings. Relying on data-driven decisions and paying close attention to customer behaviour,

Hastings recognised that there was an emerging risk to Netflix when competitors like Amazon Prime and Hulu started entering the market. Netflix was relying solely on licensed content, so there was a growing need for differentiation, and Netflix could not depend on external studios for its long-term success.

Hastings made a major transition to investing heavily in original content production, starting with the launch of *House of Cards* in 2013. By producing exclusive shows and films, Netflix reduced its reliance on third-party content, attracted more subscribers and set itself apart from competitors. This strategy also provided a hedge against rising licensing costs and the potential loss of popular shows to rival platforms.

Hastings made his third power move when the streaming market became increasingly crowded with new entrants like Disney+, Apple TV+ and HBO Max. These competitors posed a risk to Netflix's market share and subscriber growth. Hastings focused on global expansion, investing in content that resonated with diverse audiences around the world. He also continued to push for innovation in content delivery, leveraging data analytics to tailor recommendations and improve user experience. By staying ahead of competitors and continuously evolving the platform, Hastings managed the risk of losing ground in the competitive landscape. His approach to risk management at Netflix demonstrates the importance of foresight, adaptability and innovation. By recognising early signals of industry change and making bold strategic decisions, Hastings transformed Netflix from a DVD rental service into a global streaming powerhouse.

His ability to pre-empt trends has been core to the long-term success of the business.

It's one thing to 'make it', but quite another to stay the course.

Signals help us make faster, smarter decisions

We all want to make good decisions, right? Especially when people are looking to us for direction, protection and order. If we're paying attention to early signals, we can make proactive, informed decisions that position us ahead of changes rather than reacting to them.

As someone who regularly works with Australian-based businesses that have a global footprint, I'm always looking out for signals across markets. And on one summer morning in December 2019, I was particularly interested in one specific sign. I was working with the head of a major institutional bank that had a presence across 30 markets in Asia. There were very early reports about a novel coronavirus, but the signals were weak. There were reports, but they had not hit mainstream channels.

But based on information coming out of certain cities, the bank had made the decision that day to embargo travel for all staff. Looking back, this was an early and bold call. I wasn't privy to the intelligence that led to this decision, but this was when I knew that I needed to pay more attention to what was happening in China. Having people on the ground was a key driver in identifying these crucial signals of change. Well before the Christmas holiday rush, the bank could make a fast and

Engage

effective decision to safeguard its staff by asking them to stay put, minimising the risk of having hundreds of their people stuck in foreign countries, unable to return because of border closures.

High-AQ habit: Scan for signals of change

Highly adaptable thinkers consistently engage with signals of change so they can respond faster to new threats and opportunities. So how exactly do we go about this high-AQ habit?

How to create a scanning habit

Here is a playbook on scanning for signals of change that you can run on your own or with a team. The more consistently you scan, the more informed you are about emerging shifts.

Why? Because regularly gathering, analysing and interpreting signals from the external environment to identify future trends can help us anticipate change and be active players in shaping transformation before it disrupts us.

Step 1 – Scan the environment: Use a range of sources here – your own observations, Google News alerts, industry reports, academic journals and social media – to capture new ideas, behaviours, initiatives, community actions, policy positions and data points. Look for concrete examples, not general trends.

Step 2 – Run the signal through the checklist: Is it potentially surprising and specific? And what would happen if it scaled?

Step 3 – Check the signal strength: Is it a weak or strong signal? Is it a sign of an emerging trend, or a wild card? Where does it land in the categories below?

- **Weak signals:** These are early, often ambiguous indicators that suggest a possible trend or shift. They are typically not yet widespread or well understood. Weak signals require careful monitoring and analysis to determine their significance.

    For example, in the very early 2000s, the growing interest in plant-based diets was a weak signal. A few small, niche companies started producing plant-based meat alternatives, and only a limited group of health-conscious or environmentally focused consumers were paying attention. At that point, it wasn't clear that plant-based eating would gain mainstream traction. However, those paying attention to this weak signal could see the early stirrings of what later became a massive trend, with major food brands and restaurants incorporating plant-based options.

- **Strong signals:** A strong signal is undeniable and requires immediate attention because it suggests a major shift is already well underway.

A good example is the rapid adoption of electric vehicles (EVs). Over the past few years, car manufacturers, from Tesla to traditional giants like Ford and General Motors, have committed to transitioning their fleets to electric. Governments worldwide have also set regulations and goals for phasing out gas-powered cars and increasing EV infrastructure, such as charging stations. The growing consumer demand, coupled with regulatory pressure and advances like improved battery efficiency, all point to the fact that the era of electric vehicles is no longer speculative – it's happening. This strong signal shows that the automotive industry is undergoing a major shift, making it clear that businesses, suppliers and related industries need to adapt to this new reality of sustainable transportation.

- **Emerging issues:** An emerging issue is a new or developing concern that has the potential to significantly impact industries, societies or systems in the near future but hasn't yet reached mainstream awareness.

One example of an emerging issue is the ethical challenges and regulations around artificial intelligence (AI). This is an emerging issue because governments, industries and the public are beginning to grapple with its consequences, but the full implications are not yet clear. It could profoundly influence policy-making, business practices and even global economies, but the way we respond to these challenges is still in its formative stages.

- **Wild cards:** These are unexpected, low-probability events with high-impact potential. Wild cards can drastically alter the trajectory of current trends and require agile responses.

The CrowdStrike event on 19 July 2024 serves as a classic example of a wild card event – an unexpected, high-impact occurrence with far-reaching consequences. What began as a routine software update for CrowdStrike's Falcon security sensor quickly escalated into a global digital crisis. The faulty update caused widespread system crashes and reboot failures on Windows-based machines, leading to significant disruptions across various industries, including airlines, banks and retail. Over 5000 flights were grounded, and critical business operations – including the ability to pay for basic transactions – were halted worldwide.

This event is considered a wild card because it exposed the vulnerability of highly interconnected digital systems, where a single point of failure – like a software update – can trigger cascading impacts across the globe. Despite its initial unpredictability, the incident highlighted the urgent need for stronger resilience strategies in digital ecosystems and demonstrated the risks of automation and centralised IT systems.

Step 4 – So what? Ask the question: so what? How might this signal shift fundamental ways we organise ourselves, work, learn, socialise and live our lives? What are we moving from, and what are we moving towards? What if it scales? Share your findings with others and engage in discussions. This not only broadens your perspective, but also helps in validating and refining your insights. Are others seeing what you see?

Step 5 – Save and track your signals somewhere that is easy to access. This could be an internal shared drive, a notebook or an Excel spreadsheet. Even Post-it notes near your work desk. If you can take a photo of the signal, snap it and create a 'signals folder'.

High-AQ habit: Obsess over learning
From full-time to freelance: why knowledge workers need to obsess over learning

When an acquaintance of mine, Anna, turned 45, she decided she'd had enough of playing the corporate game at a large-scale

The four principles

firm where she was a seasoned human resource professional. Her tolerance for playing internal politics had expired; the unreasonable demands on her time were increasing, while her passion for the game that she'd been playing for twenty years was, at the same time, losing momentum. As was her desire to wear high heels and show up to after-work drinks any more than absolutely necessary.

The most obvious alternative option was to resign and start a small consultancy, taking on standalone freelance work to help other HR professionals deliver on transformation projects. The only issue was a simple and career-limiting one: she had been so comfortable in her role for the past seven years, and busy taking care of her kids, that she had failed to keep her skills current, or look ahead to what she might need for the future.

Before the pandemic, the workplace was reasonably simple. But by early 2024, things were far more complicated. The conversion to remote work at scale had drastically shifted the responsibilities placed on HR roles. Remote work meant new strategies for managing distributed teams, maintaining culture and ensuring employee wellbeing. There's now a stronger focus on mental health, flexibility and work-life balance, with HR needing to adapt policies accordingly. Talent management has also evolved, with recruitment, onboarding and training increasingly conducted virtually. Additionally, HR is now more involved in navigating complex health and safety regulations, addressing diversity and inclusion, and fostering adaptability in a rapidly changing environment. The pandemic accelerated digital transformation, making HR roles more data-driven and strategic than ever before.

Anna's desire to transition out of big business to go solo is an increasingly common one. As we settle back into a routine post-lockdown, the data reflects this rethinking of work life and choices. Several years ago, we started to see huge numbers of people leaving full-time jobs and registering as sole traders.

According to the Australian Bureau of Statistics (ABS), in June 2019, there were 1.5 million sole traders in Australia, which was 55,000 more than 2018. The year 2020 ushered in an explosion in this category. Between February and August 2020, the number of people who described their jobs as 'managing director' jumped a substantial 39 per cent. The trend continued: in 2022–23 the number of sole traders increased by almost 65,000 people, up by 4.2 per cent.

A similar trend is seen across the US, where many people are exiting traditional ways of working for greater flexibility, autonomy and control of their careers. Upwork's annual 'Freelance Forward' study found that across the US, nearly half of freelancers provide knowledge services: 47 per cent of all freelancers, or around 30 million professionals, provided knowledge services such as computer programming, marketing, IT and business consulting in 2023. The overall number of freelancers is up 3 per cent since 2018.

If you are a knowledge worker thinking about opting out of a full-time job, being obsessed with learning is especially relevant. Because when we dig deeper into the habits of freelancers, it's clear that they take their learning seriously – more seriously than those in secure, permanent jobs. I've always encouraged learners to adopt the attitude of a freelancer, because their unconscious commitment to staying relevant manifests in simple principles that see them looking forward, and looking to find ways to create value.

Upwork's study revealed that when asked about generative AI use in the past three months, freelancers were 2.2 times more likely than non-freelancers to say they frequently use generative AI tools. All up, 20 per cent (around 12.8 million freelancers) use generative AI tools multiple times a week compared to just 9 per cent of non-freelance workers. Over coffee, Anna confessed she knew the next twelve months were about playing catch-up; then she could exit having more confidence about competing for work against career freelancers who have learning embedded into their DNA.

The lesson is an obvious one: if we are in the business of knowledge, and we trade on our knowledge to land us the great freelance gigs, then we need to be obsessive about making sure we're upgrading our internal software every day. Learning is a standalone path to economic stability, a foundational driver of personal growth, and a lever for strengthening adaptability and resilience, so be unapologetic about it.

High-AQ habit: Obsess over learning

It's clear that our careers are getting longer, and the shelf life of skills is getting shorter, so the only way to keep up is to learn fast and adapt. But how do we know what we need to know? Here are four questions I pose to learners that can help provide direction on where to focus our efforts.

1. What is changing around you? Look at the major drivers of change (technology, environment, culture, politics, governance, health, social demographics and business) and ask yourself: which is the driver that is having/will have the most impact on the work I do? If you work in insurance, according to the PwC *Insurance 2025 and Beyond* report, the top three drivers of change are a widening trust gap, changing customer behaviour, and an increasingly tech-driven world, headed up by AI.

2. What is the strategy for your business? Is there a vision or strategy that you can access, and if so, where is the business going? What are the strategic objectives for the coming years?

3. Is your learning plan aligned? Are you positioning yourself to add value to that strategy? Will you have the skills, knowledge and expertise to deliver as the business progresses?

The four principles

> **4. What do you need to unlearn?** What skills, mindsets and behaviours are no longer useful, or fit for purpose? What can you let go of in order to free up the energy required for a new direction? Unlearning is the process of intentionally letting go of outdated knowledge, beliefs or habits to make room for new, more relevant information. For example:
> - **Old belief:** Failure is not an option. This traditional mindset views failure as a catastrophic setback, something to be avoided at all costs. It often leads to a fear of taking risks and stifles innovation.
> - **Unlearning process:** You might realise that this fear of failure is holding you back from experimenting and innovating.
> - **New belief:** Failure is a stepping stone to success. You adopt the mindset that each failure is a learning opportunity. Instead of avoiding challenges where failure is possible, you seek them out as chances to learn and grow, knowing that this approach will likely lead to greater success in the long run.

Double down on the way you learn best

There are so many ways we learn, but to summarise, we learn through a combination of these five modes. If we're going to consciously commit to learning, it's useful to know which mode(s) you naturally lean towards. Identify how you learn best and double down on that mode.

1. **Self-directed learning:** You like being alone and working at your own pace. You may naturally take the initiative to diagnose your learning priorities and identify resources. This could be as simple as scanning for a good podcast, taking an online course or watching videos. Typically, self-directed learners are self-motivated and enjoy autonomy.
2. **Classroom learning:** You like learning in a group, as in a traditional, structured learning environment where a teacher or instructor typically oversees instruction. It involves scheduled sessions, a predefined curriculum and face-to-face interactions with peers, offering a controlled setting for acquiring knowledge and skills.
3. **Peer-to-peer learning:** You like collaborative learning among equals who share knowledge and skills with one another. Peer-to-peer learning fosters active engagement, critical thinking and a deeper understanding through discussion, debate and mutual support.
4. **Social learning:** You like learning through observing and interacting with others within a community or social context. This mode leverages social networks, group dynamics and shared experiences, often using platforms like social media, forums or online communities to facilitate learning. Mentors, sponsors and advisers are also a fundamental part of social learning.
5. **Learning by doing:** You like jumping right in and learning as you go. This is a hands-on approach where

learning takes place through practical experience and active participation. Also known as experiential learning, it emphasises how we apply knowledge in real-world scenarios, fostering deeper understanding and skill retention.

Learn always, and in all ways

Every interaction we have is an opportunity for us to learn. Every win, every loss and every draw are an opportunity for us to be curious, build capability and develop personal agency. When we position ourselves as learners in everyday moments, we tend to become naturally curious about how we can advance ourselves. Learning gives us options; it helps us adapt more effectively to the increasing demands we face in life. Expanding our ability to learn (which can take many forms) expands our personal agency – our ability to act as an effective agent for ourselves, and our belief that we play an active role in how our life plays out. And expanded agency gives us more desire to learn.

Barbara Harvey is the head of learning at The Growth Faculty and believes we should never underestimate what we learn in everyday moments, but she says we need to redefine social learning to reflect what it looks and feels like in workforce education today.

'Social learning, by pure definition, has its origins in the 1800s, as identified with Karl Mager, who equated it to learning through observing others,' Harvey explains, in a 2024 interview. 'Two hundred years later social learning is equated not just with observation but with learning together, learning from each other and learning alongside others. This includes peer learning, mentorship, coaching and communities of practice. The beauty of social learning is that it yields results. Completion of courses in a social learning model trumps self-directed learning and social learning has so many secondary benefits, like greater collaboration, communication and a sense of belonging with those learning together.'

Try applying these two basic practices to your next conversation:

1. **Embrace awkward silences:** Speak less, listen more. Let awkward silences exist in conversations – don't rush to fill the space – as a way to encourage deeper consideration of subjects.
2. **Ask about process:** Never hesitate to ask how others arrived at a position or judgement. Ask people to take you through their thinking; how did they arrive at that point of view?

Learning is the ultimate competitive advantage

It's also emerging as the single point of failure for many candidates looking for knowledge work. Imagine this: you apply for a job, and the first thing the hiring manager looks for is your education. HR leaders increasingly tell me that they'll disqualify candidates from a process based on what they find here. If we haven't demonstrated a commitment to ongoing learning since our 1992 university graduation, we're out. Alt. F4. Next candidate, please.

This is a serious shift away from an over-reliance on the status attached to a traditional degree. Just because we got a masters degree in 2010 doesn't mean we're the right person for the job. What's been on the learning agenda since then? It's a subtle but undeniable signal of what business increasingly needs and values: people who demonstrate a willingness to adapt. Self-propelled learners who have a desire to go after knowledge understand new environments, foster a flexible mindset, reduce their fear of change, and drive innovation.

People who obsess over learning also create a culture where ongoing learning is the norm. Businesses cannot transform unless their people are transforming, so we need leaders who can drive change through a culture of continuous learning.

High-AQ habit: Propagate a 3D network
Build deeper and more diverse connections
Rarely can we get important work done, or promote large-scale change, in isolation. When we think about the role of our own networks in helping us be more engaged in change, we have the most compelling examples all around us in the form of the 'Wood Wide Web'.

Every day we scurry about our lives, moving around our neighbourhoods and our cities, completely unaware of the vast underground networks below us, and the remarkable way they sustain the land.

One wonderful example involves the towering Douglas fir tree. An evergreen conifer species in the pine family, it's native to Western North America, routinely rising between 20 and 100 metres above ground. Below ground, fungi connect the roots of different plants and trees, enabling them to communicate and share resources like water, nutrients and even chemical signals. These mycorrhizal networks are crucial – they allow older, more established trees to support and protect younger saplings by sharing resources. This network not only supports the growth and resilience of the vulnerable, it also helps the forest community respond to environmental stressors by enabling each tree to communicate and distribute resources.

It's quite an extraordinary system that, for example, allows trees to exchange carbon. In summer, when birch trees have an abundance of carbon, they transfer some of it to nearby Douglas firs that are shaded and less able to photosynthesise. In winter, when birches drop their leaves, Douglas firs return the favour by sharing carbon with the birches. The network also comes to the rescue during other stress events, such as drought or disease. If one tree is under attack by pests, it can send chemical signals through the network to warn neighbouring trees, allowing them to ramp up their defences. This mutual value exchange gives stability to the overall ecosystem, and promotes the survival and growth of both species, demonstrating the value of connectivity and cooperation in ecological networks.

This is just one fascinating insight to consider when we think about how we relate to others in the context of adapting and leading change. When we think about what's required to get things done it's important to recognise that we can rarely do things alone. Working with people across different departments, businesses or industries is often the least considered part of change, but it is by far the most significant, because relating to others is the catalyst to change that we are all a part of. Working together accelerates trust, strengthens relationships and moves us all towards a shared purpose. It contributes to shaping the kind of culture we're proud to be a part of.

In 2024 I interviewed Scientific Futurist Dr Catherine Ball about this. 'Mother nature has all of the answers,' she says. 'Ecosystems only exist to perform a service, or a set of services. When a species is disrupted in the ecosystem, it can be tolerated due to a term called "functional redundancy", whereby a species is not reliant on any one species, it's reliant on a complex web of multiple species. Functional redundancy occurs when different species perform the same role in an ecosystem, meaning that the loss of one species can be compensated [for] by others, preserving the ecosystem's stability.

'We can think about change in this sense; change is disturbance of the network. The laws of ecology are the laws of life, from coral reefs to elephants. Change is not only a necessary normal inside ecosystems, but it's actually something humans have evolved to do. All we have ever done is change. It's a fundamental, biological feature of being human.'

Rebuilding the network

When we think about how our human networks have been disrupted, we need to think about how we rebuild in a meaningful way. Our relationships can make or break our careers in moments of change, or when we have distance between ourselves and our colleagues. Which is why Dr Ball believes that hybrid working makes people more vulnerable to change, because it comes down to the strength of the relationships we have with the main players – and recognising who's in the ecosystem with you.

'This is really about using mother nature and looking at your life like a wildlife documentary, knowing who's who in the zoo, knowing who you can rely on in times of change, being clear on who has influence and who does not.'

Dr Ball says rebuilding a network is about asking: 'How can I be front of mind for the main players? It's not about showing up and walking the floor, it's about being front of mind when someone is writing a bid, pitching for a new piece of work.'

And in other cases, understanding when we're giving too much. 'Let's be clear on the distinction between mutualism and symbiosis. There are givers and takers. Two givers working together: that's mutualism, a mutual benefit. The giver and the taker working together, those roles might be incredibly subtle; that is not mutual, that is symbiosis. And dear reader, you may have been in a situation where you were working with someone and all they were doing was taking. That's when symbiosis slips into a parasitic relationship.'

Work has never been so fragmented and fragile. We're having fewer incidental conversations and probably showing up to less than half our usual pre-pandemic networking events. A study published in 2021 by Marissa King, a professor at the

Yale School of Management, found that professional networks shrank by approximately 17 per cent during the pandemic, but it feels more like 60 per cent to me. This drastic dialling back of interactions is having a profound impact on our access to diverse ideas, and opportunities to have unstructured conversations and collaborate. And it doesn't appear that we're finding our way back. A poll conducted by the Chartered Management Institute (CMI) found that in the post-emergency stage of the pandemic landscape, many professionals are struggling to rebuild their networks.

So we're moving in far smaller circles, further away from the office, and I strongly suspect we're avoiding conversation topics that could inadvertently 'trigger' colleagues. This is a dangerously narrow place to be, compared to pre-2020, when we were constantly bumping into a far wider range of people.

'When we were standing around the water cooler, the signal to noise ratio was usually out of balance, but at least we were still getting the signal,' says Dr Ball. 'We're not having the micro-moments that were a form of community building and knowledge sharing, so we have to double down on effort, re-establishing the stability, resilience and overall health of our own ecosystem.'

How can we go about testing the resiliency, strength and diversity of our own networks? Here's a simple high-AQ habit to consider.

High-AQ habit: Propagate a 3D network

To start assessing the diversity of your network, you can ask the following three questions:

1. Does everyone in my network look like me?
Consider the demographic and experiential diversity within your network. This question helps you reflect on whether your connections include individuals of different ages, genders, ethnicities, socioeconomic statuses and life experiences.

2. When was the last time someone disagreed with me?
Consider whether your network includes people who offer differing viewpoints, question assumptions, and push you to think differently. This question is a way to gauge whether your network encourages innovative and critical thinking. Think about the last time someone disagreed with you, or offered up an entirely new perspective. If you can't remember it happening, that's a signal that you need more diverse minds around you.

3. Am I spending 80 per cent of my time with people who have a job like mine?
Consider the diversity of professional backgrounds within your network. This question encourages you to think about whether your connections span different industries, sectors and job functions, which can provide

you with a broad range of insights and opportunities for cross-disciplinary collaboration.

These questions can start to help you evaluate whether your network is truly diverse, and identify areas where you may need to expand your connections.

4

Accept

The second step to being in a continual conversation with change

'Emotionally healthy people are very skilled at deciding how they think about what's happening to them and around them.'

Lisa Stephenson, The Coach Place

When we start paying attention to the signals of change around us and within us, we inevitably start seeing things that will bring transitions. The transition might be in the way we work, the way we live, the way we socialise or the way we learn. It could be a disruption in our personal relationships, or with our family. In many cases, these signals were in our line of sight a few years ago, but they were on the horizon. Now, when we glance up to take a closer look, they've moved drastically closer to us, and they're harder to dismiss or deny.

I think about high-AQ skills as skills that give us options. They give us more runway, more space to practise being prepared, being the pilot rather than the passenger in our lives. As change moves closer towards us, regardless of what form it takes, it provides an opportunity to examine and explore our relationship with acceptance.

Recently, after catching up with a friend over coffee, I realised that I needed to drastically shift my perspective. I had been repeating the same worries and concerns to him each time we talked, and this time I caught myself out. The past few years had been overwhelming – dealing with the pandemic, losing close friends, moving homes, my sister's battle with cancer, and back-to-back renovation projects. Though I generally consider myself upbeat, the weight of these experiences lingered. Parts of me felt broken, still trying to accept the disruption to my once structured nine-to-five routine. In quiet moments of reflection, I often felt as though I was holding on to precious fragments of something, unsure how to piece them back together. And the hardest part was that even if I could, they wouldn't fit. It was like I'd dropped a jigsaw puzzle that took a different form as it hit the ground. It was now my job to reimagine an entirely new image the jigsaw puzzle would create, and then figure out where to place the smaller pieces.

Accepting transience and imperfection
The power of a kintsugi mindset
Acceptance is the gateway for transformation and adaptation, and because ancient wisdom has long offered guidance

on transcending modern complexities and embracing change, I looked there for perspective. I came across the Japanese practice of *kintsugi* – the art of repairing broken pottery with lacquer mixed with a metal powder, often powdered gold.

This practice offers a beautiful metaphor: brokenness can become strength. Rather than discarding a broken bowl, the pieces are meticulously reassembled, and the cracks are highlighted with gold. The damage is not hidden but amplified, symbolising resilience and beauty in imperfection. *Kintsugi* teaches us that brokenness can be an opportunity for rebuilding, without pretending to be perfect.

In our fast-paced lives, we often discard things that break without a second thought. We wrap up a broken bowl in newspaper and bin it. But *kintsugi* challenges this mentality, urging us to approach broken things – whether physical objects or painful experiences – with patience and love.

In our time-deficient schedules, imagine the time and dedication involved in gathering the necessary tools and materials and repairing a broken bowl. There's kindness in this process – a deliberate decision not to discard the bowl, but to sit with it as it regains strength, and see it ultimately end up stronger, perhaps less likely to break in the same places.

Acceptance as a pathway to growth
As we think about what is changing around us, and accepting those changes, I want to encourage you to think about how *kintsugi* challenges our tightly held expectations about our

The four principles

life script. Essentially, here's an approach that says: life is messy, things break, and often don't play out the way we expected. When we have setbacks, we can practise acceptance by not only embracing imperfection as a natural part of life, but using those imperfect experiences as a source of power and endurance. The golden seams in *kintsugi* are a metaphor for resilience; they show that our struggles and healing processes are not weaknesses, but sources of strength and beauty. We can turn our shards of hurt and disappointment into something new and beautiful. If we choose, we can go beyond repair, and when we allow time and space for it, we can allow things to transform into something more beautiful that we can hold again. *Kintsugi* is linked to the philosophy of *wabi-sabi* – the acceptance that nothing stays the same forever. Things are impermanent, imperfect and incomplete.

Many of you reading this today are no doubt facing imperfect scenarios that are causing you deep concern. In the workplace, one example would be the role of artificial intelligence, and the very real impact it's likely to have on our jobs. People are sharing this issue with me privately. Some are extremely well-educated, agile thinkers with hard-earned MBAs and others are stay-at-home mothers wanting to step back into the workforce. There is no doubt that AI will have unintended consequences that we are yet to discover, but my firm position is that you should trust yourself and lean on the very human skill of adaptability, and the four principles outlined in this book. In the specific case of AI, the sooner we understand and accept the changes it will entail, the sooner we can understand what our next move is. As I mentioned earlier, there is no more dangerous time to be neutral on change than right now. The earlier we can be an active player in the way our job might alter, the faster we can rewrite our job description – before the CEO does.

And this ability to accept change – both in the external world and within ourselves – anchors us in a new form of stability. In this respect, acceptance is not passive; it is the first step towards active adaptation. By exploring and embracing the changes we can and cannot control we position ourselves for growth, innovation and new opportunities. For example, we cannot control developments in artificial intelligence, but we can control our ability to understand how it will likely impact the work we do, and find new opportunities as we work with it. The longer we dismiss or deny the growing presence of AI, the greater the delay to our own path.

Reframing as part of acceptance

Whether it's artificial intelligence or another form of disruption, 'the technique of reframing is a life skill we should all have', says Lisa Stephenson, founder of The Coach Place, in a 2024 personal interview. 'There's something very powerful that happens for us when we *consciously choose the meaning of an experience we've had, or a hypothetical one.* When we do that, we literally tell our brains how to feel.'

A Melbourne-based coach to many high-profile CEOs, Stephenson is routinely beside leaders when things go wrong, helping them manage their way through a crisis. 'Very few of us get through life without feeling broken or damaged at some point,' she says. 'We all get a turn at the hard stuff. It's how we respond to the trauma or challenges that determines how we heal and what we take with us into our next chapter. Every little crack, scar and pain point that we carry is an opportunity for us to decide the story we want to attach to it.

'Many of us are living in a really heightened state at the moment. We feel very aware of all the things that are hard and we are very focused on making sure that we keep moving forward. In the world of coaching, we believe there's never been a more important time to stop and work on ourselves [than] where we are right now. Those cracks and broken edges need healing time. Look hard at yours and take care of them. Do the work that's required to heal.

'Choose the meaning you want to give your experiences,' she says.

Imagine being more decisive about how we view the things that break, and the stories we attach to those experiences. Imagine taking the time to pick up pieces from a fallout and sitting with them quietly as we work with each of those shards to create something new. And imagine if what we create turns out to be far more beautiful and amazing than it was before it broke.

Getting out of 'the waiting place'
In Dr Seuss's *Oh, the Places You'll Go!*, the 'waiting place' is a metaphor for being stuck in a state of inaction, waiting for the

perfect conditions to move forward. In reality, many of us live in this space, telling ourselves we'll act when the time is right.

We often wait for ideal circumstances, but life rarely offers the perfect moment. Accepting that there will never be a 'right time' is essential.

As Stephenson notes, 'The waiting place is OK to visit – there are definitely times when we go, "I've just got to do survival." But what happens is most people are not living consciously each day, and they forget that they're actually in charge of when they exit.'

We tell ourselves, 'I'll wait until I have more money', or, 'I'll start when I feel more confident.' These familiar perspectives serve as barriers to progress. Stephenson says, 'You actually have to plan for it. You have to want it to happen.'

Acceptance is not about resignation; it is about taking responsibility for how we move forward. As Stephenson explains, 'Acceptance means I'm responsible for the meaning I'm giving this, for what I'm going to do next, and for what I'm going to let go of.' By confronting reality and accepting it, we empower ourselves to make changes – even when conditions are less than ideal. 'Everyone waits for a Monday,' says Stephenson, 'but there's rarely a right time in life where everything lines up.'

Recognising when it's time to leave
One of the biggest challenges of waiting for the 'right' time is that it often feels comfortable. We become so familiar with the reasons we can't move forward that they become part of our story. These reasons are usually based in reality – we may be dealing

with limited resources, life transitions, emotional exhaustion – but they also keep us stuck.

While waiting for the 'right' conditions, many of us forget that change is within our control. The key is realising that you've stayed in the waiting place for too long. Often, Stephenson notes, people only leave the waiting place after something forces them out, like a crisis or burnout. 'Most people only get out of the waiting place because there's a trigger for it,' she says. 'The very best time to create change is when things feel pretty good, actually.'

Moving forward with small, consistent steps

Leaving the waiting place doesn't require a dramatic overhaul of your life. Stephenson reminds us that change doesn't come all at once, but rather through small, intentional actions that keep us moving forward.

'People make everything bigger than it needs to be,' she says. 'What are the small things I can do right now?' Whether it's spending fifteen minutes a day on a new goal or reaching out to someone in your network for a conversation, these small steps add up over time. 'You just need to do acceptance, be responsible, and each day think about what's one thing I can do today to shift forward.'

In today's world, where uncertainty has become the norm, it's easy to fall into the trap of waiting – for better conditions, more certainty, a clearer path ahead. But as Stephenson's insights show, the waiting place is not where we're meant to stay. Acceptance is not about giving in to the current circumstances, but about taking responsibility for how we move through them. By making small, deliberate choices, we can shift our lives out of stagnation and begin to create meaningful change.

As Stephenson puts it, 'When I change, everything around me changes.' The lesson for us today is to stop waiting for the perfect moment and instead take action, however small, to start adapting and actively shaping our future.

> ### Principle #2: Accept what we can (and cannot) change
>
> True power lies in understanding what is changing, and what we can and cannot influence. By accepting the evolving conditions around and within us, we prepare ourselves to explore new possibilities.
>
> **The high-AQ habits that support this principle are:**
> - run a values audit
> - detect impermanence
> - conduct a resilience reality check
> - apply the 'good advice' test.

High-AQ habit: Run a values audit

In times of uncertainty and change, understanding our core values becomes essential to navigating life's complexities, and may serve as a starting point in exiting the waiting place. Stephenson stresses the importance of conducting a 'values audit' – a process of identifying and reaffirming our top non-negotiable values. This audit serves as a personal compass, helping us make decisions that are aligned with what truly matters to us. In Stephenson's words, 'If you don't know what your five non-negotiable values are and you can't articulate them and roll them off your tongue, the consequence is that other people tell you what's important.'

A values audit is about clarifying what we stand for, what we are willing to fight for, and what we are not willing to compromise. Stephenson explains, 'Your non-negotiable values are your filtering system. They tell you what you're going to say yes to and what you're going to say no to.' This framework allows us to make decisions that are not only strategic but also deeply aligned with who we are. I've always said that when we're grounded in our values, decisions come faster and easier – because our actions are coming from our source of truth.

High-AQ habit: Run a values audit

When facing a decision, use the values audit to ensure your choices align with what matters most to you. Follow these steps:

1. **Identify your core values**: Think of your top three to five non-negotiable values. These could be integrity, growth, family, creativity or service, for example. Be clear on what drives and anchors you.

2. **Evaluate the decision**: Ask yourself:
    - Does this decision support or conflict with my core values?
    - Am I making this choice because it's true to me, or because it's expected by others?
3. **Filter the options**: For each possible choice, apply these three filters:
    - **Alignment**: Does this path align with my core values?
    - **Impact**: Will this decision positively affect the things I value most?
    - **Long-term fit**: Will this choice still feel right years from now?
4. **The gut check**: Trust your intuition – does this choice feel like it aligns with who you are, or does it bring discomfort?

Example: If 'family' is one of your core values, and you're considering a new job that offers great pay but will significantly reduce time spent with loved ones, the values audit might highlight that this decision is not in line with your priorities.

High-AQ habit: Detect impermanence

I recently found myself playing a game of Bananagrams with some friends' kids at a café. For the uninitiated, Bananagrams is like Scrabble, but without the board – you get a set number of letters and have to make your own grid of words, and you can change the grid as often as you like, to come up with better word combinations. The idea is to use up your allocation of letters, and the first person to do so calls 'Peel!', which means each player has to pick up a new letter. It's a dynamic game where the environment is constantly changing with the addition of new letters.

I was going strong, calling 'Peel!', adding to my grid and feeling proud of my vocabulary. But I soon got stuck with a tricky letter and fell behind, accumulating letters I couldn't do much with as my fellow players steamed ahead. It soon became clear that I needed to abandon my masterpiece and rebuild my grid, rather than trying to add on to or tweak my words with each random letter that came in. Yet I found myself feeling attached to the words I'd created – I didn't want to start again!

While this might seem like a very inconsequential example, it's an interesting lesson in how easy it is to become attached to what's around us, or what we know. When I did finally blow up my Bananagrams, I created a much better version – but I was too late, and my ten-year-old opponents were faster (the neuroplasticity of a younger brain in action!).

Accepting change starts with recognising the reality of impermanence. It's a concept we're all familiar with, but often struggle to reconcile. Like me with my Bananagrams, we sometimes get stuck because we become attached to what is – or how we think something *should* be. As I'll continue to explore throughout this book, nature provides us with many poignant metaphors and lessons on how to live harmoniously and in synchronicity with change. And it rehearses acceptance routinely, every day, every season – as frequently as conditions demand.

A striking example of impermanence is the Japanese cherry blossom tree, or *sakura*. *Sakura* blossoms are renowned for their breathtaking beauty, but their blooming period is extremely short – usually only a week or two in spring, when conditions are perfect. This perfect impermanence reminds us of the power of acceptance. Like everything in nature, its cycles align seamlessly with conditions it can't control.

The Japanese have a phrase to articulate the beauty in transience. In Japanese culture, *sakura* trees are associated with the concept of *mono no aware*, an idea that emphasises the beauty in transience and the acceptance of change. The practice of *hanami*, or flower viewing, celebrates the fleeting beauty of the *sakura* and the acceptance of change. The concepts of *mono no aware* and *hanami* serve as poignant metaphors for accepting the transience of life, and also the power of presence: once we accept that all things are subject to change, we can practise true presence, appreciating moments or things without fear of losing them. Many of us are so busy replaying our past and predicting our future that we lose the ability to ground ourselves in the moment without the clouds of past hurt informing future fear.

What are you resisting?

Impermanence is one of the foundational beliefs in Buddhism and underscores the acceptance of the transient, changeable and perishable nature of everything in the physical and mental world.

The four principles

As with my game of Bananagrams, we can all use small moments to recognise where resisting impermanence is actually holding us back. By giving yourself time and space to objectively assess how the signals of change that you learned to identify in the previous chapter are impacting the environment or conditions around you, you can see where you're resisting change, resisting impermanence.

> ### High-AQ habit: Detect impermanence
>
> Think back to times when you believed something would last – it could be a physical item, a relationship or a belief. For example, many of us invested in DVD collections, only to see streaming services replace them within a decade. This highlights how easily we misjudge the permanence of things.
>
> Now, apply this thinking to your life:
> - Are you resisting change in any area – relationships, work or habits – because you're holding on to a sense of permanence? (Thinking things will stay the same just because that's how they've been.)
> - Have you invested time, money or energy into something that is now holding you back, but don't want to let it go because of the 'sunk cost fallacy' (where you're reluctant to let something go because of the investment you've made, even when you can see letting it go will be beneficial).

> Now consider the signals of change you've identified in your current environment. Challenge any assumptions of permanence, and take one small step to let go. For example, if you haven't exercised in a while, start with just a five-minute routine instead of waiting for the perfect moment to begin an exercise regimen.

Why blind acceptance is easy – and should be avoided

Until Roger Bannister ran the mile in under four minutes in 1954 (the first time the feat was officially recorded), doctors, biomechanics experts and scientists said that the human body was not capable of breaking that time barrier; that the body couldn't withstand the stress of running at such a pace over that distance. Less than two months after Bannister's historic run, Australian athlete John Landy repeated the 'impossible' feat, and shaved 1.5 seconds off Bannister's time. Around 50 more athletes ran the mile in under four minutes that same year, and thousands of athletes have done so since.

American civil rights activist Marian Wright Edelman popularised the phrase: 'You can't be what you can't see', and the story of the four-minute mile demonstrates this concept. Once Bannister broke the barrier, the floodgates opened for athletes who believed it was possible because they had seen it.

The story highlights an important point: it's critical that we don't accept things blindly. We must apply filters to decide what

The four principles

it is that we are willing to accept, and what requires us to think more critically. It also gives us some insights into the way humans operate, the impact of the environment, and the concept of pre-attentive processing.

Pre-attentive processing is the subconscious accumulation of information from the environment which our brains use to filter and process what is important. All information that enters our consciousness is pre-attentively processed, and assumptions like the impossibility of a four-minute mile – particularly when supported by 'scientific evidence' and expert opinion – can have profound impacts on what we accept as truth.

In her 2016 book, *How to Have a Good Day: Think Bigger, Feel Better and Transform Your Working Life*, economist and former McKinsey consultant Caroline Webb applies a behavioural science lens to wisdom, or making good decisions, and talks about the importance of engaging our brain's deliberate system when we're dealing with things that matter.

Webb explains that the deliberate system is the network that manages analysis, self-discipline and forward thinking – all skills we engage when exercising judgement. The downside of not consciously engaging this system is that the automatic system subtly takes over, defaulting to the easiest solution available. It does this to conserve energy, which is an important function to avoid decision fatigue, but if you rely on this system for important decisions in your career or life, you could end up with the wrong choice.

Webb recommends looking out for signs that indicate your automatic system is in charge, including:

- Someone shuts down the idea because it's the easiest option.
- 'Let's just do what's always worked.'
- 'My friend told me this, therefore …'
- 'We don't have the time or the money for that.'

Conscious effort to activate our deliberate processing system helps direct the effect of pre-attentive processing when we're considering new information or signals of change. We must evaluate signals, beliefs and assumptions critically to decide how much meaning we attribute to them, how much we take on, and what parts we can control. This starts with accepting the things that we cannot control in order to invest our energy in the things that we can.

The 'upper limit' theory

Going back to the four-minute mile story, I'm reminded of Gay Hendricks's work on the upper limit theory in his 2009 book, *The Big Leap: Conquer Your Hidden Fear and Take Life to the Next Level*. Hendricks proposes that we all have subconscious barriers that prevent us from achieving our full potential, and that these self-imposed ceilings cap our success, happiness and growth. Essentially, we will often meet the limits we or others set for us, conscious or not, just as we will often chase definitions of success that we did not come up with, because our environment presents them as the most obvious path.

These examples show us that we must consciously and deliberately evaluate the signals, beliefs and conditions we take on. Acceptance is foundational to transformation and adaptation, but we must be aware of unconscious or blind acceptance.

High-AQ habit: Conduct a resilience reality check
Balancing hope with a broken heart

If you're in the business of keeping people safe at work, then you are probably familiar with the role of a 'safety share' at the start of a meeting or shift. It's a short discussion that highlights safety practices, incidents or near misses. Its role is to raise awareness, encourage learning from real-life examples, and promote open dialogue about safety concerns. It reinforces best practices and helps foster a safety-first culture by keeping safety top of mind. I am often privy to these rather powerful and personal discussions with clients and their teams, and one safety share in particular, the Stockdale paradox, has real relevance to each of us, as we consider the role of 'acceptance' along our journey.

It was shared during lockdown by one of the mining industry's leaders in the field of learning and development, Brendan Howard. A former geologist, Howard has been building capability in leaders across Rio Tinto for 30 years. Part of his role is to help build a culture of technical excellence in Rio Tinto, to enable the company to safely achieve its goals. This means challenging the mindsets of roughly 10,000 engineers and scientists around the world. As part of this process, Howard used my program, Adaptive Leadership. (This entire book is a result of the work we have done with Rio Tinto since 2021.)

The Stockdale paradox

The Stockdale paradox is a concept that revolves around balancing two seemingly contradictory ideas. Named after Admiral James Stockdale, a Vietnam War prisoner who survived over seven years of captivity, this mindset was key to his survival. He didn't just rely on blind optimism or stoic resignation. Instead, he combined a clear-eyed view of his harsh reality with a deep belief that he would eventually make it through. This paradox is more than just a historical footnote – it's a practical and deeply relevant mindset that we can all apply when navigating life's toughest moments.

At its heart, the Stockdale paradox is about maintaining a delicate balance between two ideas:

- Have unwavering faith that you will eventually overcome whatever challenge you're facing, no matter how difficult it gets.
- Simultaneously, confront the brutal facts of your current reality, without sugar-coating or avoiding them.

On the surface, this may sound like a contradiction. How can you be both hopeful and brutally honest at the same time? But that's precisely the point.

When reflecting on his time as a prisoner of war, Stockdale

was interviewed by leadership expert and author Jim Collins for his iconic 2001 book, *Good to Great*. When asked, 'Who didn't make it out?', his response was revealing. He said that the *optimists* were the ones who *didn't* survive. They were the prisoners who kept saying things like, 'We'll be out by Christmas', or 'We'll be out by Easter', and when those dates came and went, they became demoralised and eventually gave up hope.

Stockdale said these prisoners 'died of a broken heart' because their unrealistic optimism couldn't sustain them through the harsh and uncertain reality of their situation. He emphasised the importance of balancing optimism with confronting the brutal facts of the present; maintaining hope for the future, while accepting the reality of the moment, no matter how difficult it is.

Why acceptance of your reality matters

Acceptance is a huge part of the Stockdale paradox, but it's not the kind of acceptance that means giving up or passively letting things happen. It's about being brutally honest with yourself about what's going on right now. Whether it's a difficult relationship, a challenging work situation, or even a global crisis, we've all been in situations where denial feels like the easier option. But as Stockdale's story shows, ignoring reality only makes things worse in the long run.

When we talk about acceptance, we're talking about looking at the facts without filtering them through wishful thinking or avoidance. Think about it with respect to your own life: maybe you're facing a career setback, or you're going through a rough patch in a relationship. It's tempting to think, 'Things will get better soon' without doing the hard work of facing what's actually happening. Stockdale's philosophy teaches us that the only way out is through. If we're not honest about where we are, we can't take the necessary steps to move forward.

Acceptance gives you power. When you face the truth of your situation head-on, you take control of what you can. Stockdale accepted the brutality of his imprisonment, but didn't let it crush him. He used that clarity to focus on survival.

The role of hope

But acceptance alone isn't enough. The second part of the Stockdale paradox is just as important: hope. You need to believe that, no matter how tough things get, you will eventually make it to the other side. This isn't blind optimism or wishful thinking, though. Stockdale wasn't telling himself, 'I'll be out by next week' or, 'Everything will magically get better.' His hope was grounded in his belief in his own resilience – his ability to endure whatever came his way, for however long it took.

This type of hope is practical. It's about trusting yourself and your capacity to handle difficulties, even when the timeline for improvement is uncertain. It's not about setting arbitrary deadlines, or pretending everything will be fine by a certain date. Instead, it's about believing that, in the long run, you have what it takes to prevail.

The four principles

Why the Stockdale paradox is relevant today
We're living in a time of constant uncertainty and change, whether it's personal challenges or broader societal shifts. It's easy to get caught between unrealistic optimism and bleak resignation. Stockdale's approach reminds us that it's not about choosing one or the other. It's about holding both: accepting where you are, while believing in where you're going.

This mindset can shift our axis of thinking when it comes to practising acceptance, which is the first step towards taking action. When you face the facts of your situation, you can make informed decisions, take steps to improve things, and eventually overcome the challenges in front of you. At the same time, keeping hope alive – hope based in your own strength and resilience, not just wishful thinking – keeps you moving forward. It motivates you to keep going, even when the road is long and hard. Acceptance and hope aren't opposing forces – they work together to help you survive and thrive, no matter what life throws at you.

High-AQ habit: Conduct a resilience reality check

A daily resilience practice involves two key steps:
1. **Reality check:** Acknowledge the current facts, both good and bad, without sugar-coating. Identify what isn't working.
   For example: 'This project is behind schedule, and I'm feeling overwhelmed and overloaded about the growing

Accept

list of tasks. There are still several unknowns, and I'm not sure how I'll meet the deadline. It's clear I have a lot on my plate, and I need to get clarity from my team on a few issues.'

2. **Resilience reflection**: Focus on your ability to handle the challenges ahead. Reflect on past successes and remind yourself that you can prevail. This practice balances acceptance with optimism, reinforcing both the harshness of reality and the strength to overcome it.

   For example: 'I've faced tight deadlines before and found a way through by breaking things down and tackling them step by step. Today, I'll focus on getting clarity on those unknowns and prioritising the tasks that need immediate attention. I've been here before. I know I have the skills and experience to handle this. I'll take one step at a time and trust that I can make steady progress. I can ask for help if I need to, from any of my mentors, colleagues or team members.'

By practising this daily habit, you can strengthen your ability to both accept the harshness of your current reality and maintain a resilient mindset for the future.

High-AQ habit: Apply the 'good advice' test

The best piece of advice I ever got was from my journalism professor at university in 1994. He told me that if I got out of my tracksuit pants, I could go anywhere in the world, and do anything I wanted. And he was right. Dr Peter Young's firm counsel set fire to my eighteen-year-old mind, lighting it up with the possibilities of different futures I could go after. It was advice that I believed without hesitation, because he had my best interests at heart. It prompted me to think differently. And I knew that if I took his advice, we'd both win.

Today, as we work through accepting both opportunities and setbacks in our lives, we often lean on those around us for advice. And these days it's available in unlimited amounts – there are many people handing out aggressive opinions positioned as advice on how to run every part our lives. Some of it is actually profound. Most of it isn't. But I think we can all agree that advice culture is a noisy, overwhelming space. So how can we distinguish between good and bad advice, especially in moments of transition?

> ### High-AQ habit: Apply the 'good advice' test
>
> *What good advice really looks like*
> I'm getting asked for advice more frequently, which has prompted me to reflect on what good advice really is, because I know my take on things can often be swift and unintentionally brutal. When I was researching this, my first call was to Lisa Stephenson. 'As adults, we are

Accept

attached to three things,' she said. We are attached to advice that:
- makes us right
- makes us look good
- makes us feel comfortable.

Sometimes talking to a like-minded person is all that's required. But advice is not really advice when it only validates what we are already thinking. Good advice has the following qualities:
- It should be confronting.
- It should make us think differently.
- It should make us sit back and want to ask more questions.

Good advice should be tested

When someone shares what you think is good advice with you, Stephenson thinks you should test it by asking questions like, 'Why do you have that view?', or 'What experience have you had that makes you think that?' This can be a useful baseline for advice that we're offered today.

I have three questions that I'll add to Stephenson's list, because unfortunately, in this complicated life, I've come to realise that not everyone wants to see you do well – even people close to you. Not everyone wants you to find your version of happiness. Consider these questions:

- Is the advice autobiographical? (Does this person have a perspective that expands or limits their ability to provide personal counsel?)
- Does this person truly have my best interests at heart?
- Who wins if I take this advice?

Don't ask for advice when you don't need it

Don't create unnecessary noise by seeking advice when you don't need it. Information overload undermines the personal agency required to do what we actually want to do. We're already dealing with a laundry list of daily overwhelm, including email, social media and curating our news feeds, just as a starting point. Don't pile onto this list with additional noise if your instinct on something is strong.

Personal agency is the ability to act as an effective agent for ourselves; to reflect, make effective decisions and construct a meaningful life. And it starts with what we let into our mind. When we control our exposure to external stimuli, we improve the clarity of our thinking, our judgement and our overall quality of life.

And remember, advice comes at us in many forms, but mostly from people in our immediate circle. So the link between the quality and usefulness of the advice we receive and the company we keep is an obvious one. Our relationships are critical to our sense of agency – or lack thereof. When we associate selectively, when we surround ourselves with people who encourage us to reach our full potential (while also seeking out diverse perspectives), we develop confidence that extends to other parts of our lives.

Acceptance and the 'adjacent possible'

The 'adjacent possible' refers to the set of all possible next steps or innovations that are one step away from the current state of things. It's a theory popularised by author Steven Johnson in his 2010 book, *Where Good Ideas Come From: The Natural History of Innovation.*

Any good advice should act as a pointer to new possibilities in our life – new pathways that give us energy and agency to love life just that little bit more.

In our fast-moving world, waiting for perfect conditions is a trap. Acceptance is not about giving in but about taking responsibility for how we move through difficult circumstances. By practising acceptance, we create a pathway to meaningful change, one small, deliberate move at a time.

5

Activate

The third step to being in a continual conversation with change

---

'Dreams always come before reality. Before something can exist, it must be built. Before it can be built, it must be planned. And before it can be planned, it must be imagined.'
James McCrae, *The Art of You: The Essential Guidebook for Reclaiming Your Creativity*

I had what I considered a normal childhood, growing up in the western Queensland town of Goondiwindi. I was one of three girls, the middle child. We had a house, two cars and a dog – that was my interpretation of what 'normal' looked like. But we did know that our father wasn't like other dads. He didn't seem to have a traditional job; he seemed to make his own rules, and no one ever told him what to do. There was no chance anyone was going to supervise my father.

The four principles

Dad left school before graduating and, from a very young age, he ran a fast-growing trucking haulage business in remote regional Queensland, transporting materials across extreme distances. Inevitably, trucks and tankers would break down and the most efficient way to get spare parts to them was to fly them out, routinely landing on a very remote highway where there was rarely any traffic to avoid. We didn't really know what this meant, but we did know that no one else's dad did things like this during their day.

The huge upside to this was that Dad had his pilot's licence from a very young age. And lucky for us, this meant we really looked forward to school holidays. Dad would unfold an enormous navigational map across the dining room table and pose one simple question: 'Where do you want to go?'

My answer was always: everywhere.

Imagine that – having no limits on where you could go as young, impressionable girls, curious about the world. Only now do I truly recognise what those moments meant. That one simple question meant far more than making a plan for the school holidays. It was a provocation to create our own future, an invitation to use our imagination, and a moment to think about what was possible in our little lives. It was the earliest and most powerful lesson on the role of personal agency. It established a core belief that we could set an objective and go after it. We could co-create our own future, if we were prepared to engage our imagination. We didn't default to someone else's picture of the future. There were no limits, no constraints. The possibilities were endless – that's certainly how it felt then, and how I feel today.

And we were all-in on this remarkable opportunity. We came up with our own flight plan, measuring the distance between towns and watching Dad write down details in his logbook. All maps and flying collateral lived in his flight bag, which he still has. When we saw the flight bag on the floor of his office, we knew he was going somewhere.

On every single trip, we were utterly captivated by the landscapes that formed this lucky country. We visited Uluru, soared through the many islands that pepper the Great Barrier Reef, and hugged the Snowy Mountains in the back of a single-engine light aircraft, never afraid of the bumps along the way. Turbulence was part of the journey. Dad used to explain to us that we never had to be concerned about bouncing around as we flew through clouds. The clouds were constantly changing, he told us. They were forming and reforming, which meant they were generating energy, and we had to ride out that change. But once we got clear of the cloud, we were fine.

It was an early metaphor for life: you can't always avoid bad weather, but you can be slightly more at ease with it when you see it ahead of you on the horizon and decide how to minimise the crosswinds.

'Only pack what you can carry' was Dad's strict rule as we prepared for each trip. This is still a family mantra, and a joke that comes up randomly over long lunches today. Another early and profound metaphor for life: only take what you need; let go of things that you don't need. You won't need those things for where we're going. Whatever we need, we'll pick up on the way.

The role of imagination

Only today, as I study the field of futures thinking, do I understand the value of these early lessons, especially in the conversation about activating our optimism and energy for change.

For me, a fundamental piece of activating ourselves and preparing for change is understanding the role and power of our imagination. If we forego the chance to imagine our own future, then we'll unconsciously default to someone else's. For example, if you google images of 'the future of food', you'll see a lot of robots making perfectly portioned meals, green coloured steak and a disproportionate number of skewered insects. This is not my future of food, and I sincerely doubt it's yours.

Reanna Browne is a futurist who you'll remember from Chapter 2, 'Modern success metrics'. 'How we think about the future shapes what we do in the present,' she says. 'But it also shapes what we think is possible.' We have to remember: 'There is no data on the future, because the future has not happened. We only have data on the past (what has happened), data on the present (what is happening) and data on the ideas, projections and images of the future. This informs our ability to plan, and make sense of change. Futures work is about our actions in the present.'

Browne and I talk constantly about what good futures work looks like, and it always comes back to 'personal agency' and posing the question: how much influence do I believe I have over the future?

More agency, more options

Hopefully, you are already feeling like you have far greater influence over the way you experience change and anticipate your future. When we practise the principles of *Adapt*, we not only adapt more effectively to change, we strengthen our personal agency. Agency is the highest form of personal competence, because this is what enables us to make effective decisions about how to adapt to more demands and changing situations. We can be capable or empowered – but agency is what activates us to take control of our mindset in small and big moments.

Performance coach Ben Crowe talked about the importance of this on Dominic Price's *Experts Unleashed* podcast. A week before his wedding, Price had a lot happening in his household. His family had arrived from the UK and his twins were running madly around the kitchen when the discovery was made that no one had turned on the dishwasher the night before. With a house full of guests looking for clean coffee mugs, this could have been an explosive moment for some. 'Well, no one's died here,' said Price. That was a micro example of where agency kicks in. Crowe says, 'Agency is the ability to decide how to interpret the events of our life in real time. Most of us don't realise we have that power.'

Personal agency is also vital in the larger moments. If we're made redundant, for example, agency is what allows us to not let the conditions of our environment determine our perspective in the moment. We get to decide how it makes us feel; how to move through it.

Agency will play an increasingly important role in our lives, particularly as we face more change more often, which can leave us feeling as though we won't be able to keep up or fully adapt to what comes next. It's so easy to exist in the silent chaos of worry that we're not doing what we're meant to do. And the anxiety we feel in these moments makes it difficult to get things done, creating a spiral of inaction. What we need is a higher sense of agency: the ability to cut through all of what pulls at us, find emotional and physical balance, think more clearly, and advocate for ourselves, so we can take a course of action that makes sense and feels good.

When we have a high sense of agency, we create clear pathways to a preferred future.

'This is about gaining clarity, not certainty,' says Browne. 'It's not about making predictions, it's about saying, "What is changing around us, how could that play out – and *now* what does that mean I will do in the present?"' says Browne. She encourages us to consider these simple questions: 'What?', 'So what?' and 'Now what?':

- **What is changing? What might happen? What have we assumed?**

  For example, what is changing across the workplace or industry? What are the signals we have been paying attention to? Are we headed for a restructure in our workplace in the short term?

- **What does this mean for us? Where do we want to grow?** Is this an opportunity to reimagine a new job or career? Is this an opportunity to reach out to old ties and make new connections? Is this a chance to re-evaluate my skills and learn something new?
- **What will we do now?** If direction is more important than speed, can I take time to experiment with new options or side hustles to narrow down what might be the next move?

> ### Principle #3: Activate
>
> Be an active player in change by activating your energy and optimism for the new. Pursue new pathways to your preferred future. Imagine how change can play out, without constraints. Consider how you can deliberately create space to imagine what's possible.
>
> **The high-AQ habits that support this principle are:**
> - exploration versus exploitation
> - test the truth
> - run 'what if' scenarios.

High-AQ habit: Exploration over exploitation
The secret life of bees

Rory Sutherland shares a terrific story in his 2022 keynote, 'The Magic of Original Thinking', to illustrate the extraordinary

The four principles

benefits of exploration. The advertising guru uses a lesser-known fact about bees to land his point.

In the hive system, worker bees leave the hive to explore the surrounding environment, searching for nectar and pollen from flowers. Once they locate a good source, they return to the hive and communicate the distance and location to other bees through what's known as the waggle dance.

But not all bees take notice. Scientists discovered that about 20 per cent of bees ignore the waggle dance; they dismiss the directions and go off at random, which doesn't make any sense, because if you want to maximise the efficiency of pollen collection, you'd want 100 per cent obedience to the waggle dance. 'Bees have this indulgent class of bees who are allowed to make mistakes,' says Sutherland.

And then scientists discovered what was happening. In all dynamic systems, including animal foraging, there is an explore/exploit trade-off. These systems need a trade-off between exploiting what they already know (in the case of the beehive, for example, that there are flowers over the hill from which they've been successfully getting pollen for the past two weeks) and investing in what they don't yet know. So the bees that ignored the waggle dance were the explorers, setting out to forage for new sources of pollen to keep the hive alive.

'This is why we need to invest in the things you don't yet know, either because the future is different from the past or because, simply, you have not discovered it yet,' says Sutherland.

This is why we need to be exploring and working on projects where we're allowed to fail 10 to 20 per cent of the time, just like the explorer bee cohort.

It makes sense for the beehive: 'If you don't have a certain variation built into the system, you become over-optimised on the past and the hive starves to death,' says Sutherland. 'And you never get lucky, either. You don't have a system that allows you to exploit lucky discoveries, or even lucky mistakes.'

> ### High-AQ habit: Exploration versus exploitation
>
> This is a lesson we see replayed in business time and time again. When an organisation or individual is too busy exploiting their success, while not exploring new possibilities, they aren't paying attention to what is about to disrupt them. So how can we prioritise exploration over exploitation in our own lives?
>
> 1. **Be clear on the definitions.**
>
>   *Exploration* involves trying new tools, techniques or strategies that you haven't used before. It's about learning and discovering new possibilities that could enhance your adaptability.
>
>   *Exploitation* means making the most of the tools and techniques you already know and are comfortable with. It's about refining and optimising what you're already good at.

2. **Be clear about what adaptability means to you.**
   Define what adaptability means in your context. Is it about responding to change faster, being more innovative or better managing uncertainty? Your goal will guide whether you need more exploration or exploitation.
3. **Have an 80/20 rule.**
   Dedicate a specific portion of your time to exploring new tools. For example, you might allocate 20 per cent of your time to learning and experimenting with new techniques or technologies.
4. **Embrace the small moves in a long game.**
   Test new tools on a small scale before fully committing. This allows you to explore without abandoning what's already working. If a tool shows promise, gradually increase its use.
5. **Diversify your exploration.**
   Don't just explore tools or have conversations within your current domain. Look at how different industries or disciplines approach adaptability, for example by borrowing ideas from outside your field or showing up to industry conferences that aren't related to the work you do.
6. **Avoid the comfort trap.**
   If you find yourself repeatedly using the same tools out of habit, it's time to prioritise exploration.

> Comfort can hinder adaptability, as it may prevent you from seeing the need for change until it's too late.

High-AQ habit: Test the truth
From 'soldiering on' to staying home

Remember when, before 2020, in many workplaces, if you had a cold it was ridiculous to not go to work? We toughened up, battled through and got on with business as usual. It was considered normal to show up to the office with all the symptoms of a cold along with a box of tissues and be the all-day recipient of both supportive and sarcastic remarks about your level of dedication to the cause.

Things are very different in the present day, where even the hint of a cough or sore throat means not only staying home but avoiding contact with anyone, and possible at-home Covid testing, in case you unintentionally infect anyone else. The social norm has been rewritten; it's now ridiculous to go to work if you have a cold.

This is a simple and powerful example of how change happens, how fast things can change and the danger of assuming that things will always be the same.

'The future often arrives through the unexpected and even the ridiculous,' says Reanna Browne. 'Our actions are guided by images and assumptions about what lies ahead – most of them unexamined, borrowed from the world around us.

The four principles

These visions aren't always ours alone; they're shaped by powerful voices, familiar ideas and cultural expectations. Often, they feel comfortable, keeping us anchored in what we already know and subtly shrinking our sense of possibility. These familiar visions limit our imagination, quietly defining what we consider possible – and what we don't. But these influences don't just come from loud declarations. They're embedded in subtle norms, shared stories, and the background patterns that influence us as much as we shape them.'

What is true today may not necessarily be true forever, or even tomorrow.

'Testing the truth' is a common practice in the field of futures thinking and is a valuable technique that involves taking established facts or assumptions and deliberately reversing them to explore alternative scenarios and possibilities. This activity wakes up our imagination, inviting us to move beyond the obvious and imagine entirely new possibilities. Testing today's facts challenges our mental models about how things will work in the future.

The fast version of this high-AQ habit is simple: when you are confronted with a truth, challenge yourself to consider: will this be true forever? How might this be different in a few years?

The longer version is the following and it can serve as a thought-provoking activity for your team, if you need to break open fixed thinking about the way things have always been done.

Activate

High-AQ habit: Test the truth

1. **Choose a topic:** For example, 'the future of gambling'.
2. **Make a list of everything that you know to be true:** For example, major horse races are common, casinos are common, cash is 50 per cent of gaming revenue, there are public holidays in some states that celebrate major games, competition and races.
3. **Test the truth:** What is the opposite of everything you've written down? Rewrite each fact with the opposite in mind, for example, racecourses are used for new housing developments, casinos are out of date, we operate in a cashless society, younger generations don't believe in gambling, government removes gambling licences because of changing community expectations, lowest turnout on record for the annual Melbourne Cup.
4. **Google search the new truth:** What do you find? Pockets of signals where the flipped future facts are already true? Why and how did this change happen? What's it like to live in this new world? What does this mean for the risks and opportunities that are not obvious when we only consider conventional scenarios? What does this mean for your future practice? (If we never retire, how do we engage learning practices that keep us employable?) Which direction is our ideal direction to head towards?

This was a real-world scenario in a workshop I was running. These facts may not concern you, but if you're the CEO of a gambling business where half of your revenue comes from cash on major horse racing days I would argue that these signals of change should have been taken seriously many years ago.

By testing these scenarios, you prepare yourself and your organisation to be more adaptable, because you are exploring the consequences of these reversed assumptions. Adopting a habit as simple as this one can reveal alternative paths and strategies, making you more resilient in the face of unexpected changes.

'Remember when we held a single job for life, or when remote work was a radical idea?' asks Browne. 'Looking back, we can recognise the absurdity of our past and make room for the possibility that what seems unimaginable and ridiculous today could become normal tomorrow.'

High-AQ habit: Run 'what if' scenarios
Unilever's bold approach to sustainability
A masterclass in adaptive leadership involves the former CEO of Unilever, Paul Polman. Under his direction in 2010, the global leader in consumer goods launched an ambitious plan called the Unilever Sustainable Living Plan. At its core, this plan was based on the simple yet powerful concept of scenario planning, asking key questions like, *'What if* the future demands businesses to operate sustainably?' This question was key in driving the company's strategy to achieve long-term growth while reducing its environmental impact. By proactively addressing potential

environmental challenges, Unilever set a new standard for corporate responsibility. Polman was (and still remains) relentless in his quest for sustainability. On LinkedIn, he explains: 'With a tremendous team, we embraced a longer-term, purpose-driven approach that put the business in service of all our stakeholders: employees, customers, suppliers, the communities we touched, plus the planet and the next generation.'

Polman understood what it truly meant to be an active player in change – to lead change and pre-empt change. To anticipate and influence change. He was paying attention to the signals of change. Which is why he was relentless in posing the question: *'What if?'*

He provoked his team to move beyond the obvious, explore potential futures and essentially ask, 'What role does Unilever want to play in a future where things will look very different?'

The challenge: a changing global landscape and consumers who expect more

The early 2000s marked a significant shift in consumer behaviour. Awareness about environmental sustainability was rising, with increasing concerns about climate change, resource depletion and the social impact of business operations. In addition to evolving consumer preferences, governments were implementing stricter regulations on environmental practices, creating more pressure on businesses to reduce their ecological footprints.

For Unilever, which owns well-known brands like Dove, Lipton and Ben & Jerry's, the stakes were high. As one of the world's largest producers of food, beverages, personal care products and home goods, Unilever had a substantial impact on the environment. The company recognised that continuing business as usual was no longer an option.

The 'what if' scenario: planning for a sustainable future

Unilever's leadership, led by Paul Polman at the time, began to ask the crucial question: 'What if consumers and governments demand more sustainable business practices?' They knew that to remain competitive in the future, they had to align the company's operations with the growing demand for environmental responsibility.

This led to the creation of the Unilever Sustainable Living Plan, a bold initiative designed to achieve three primary goals:

1. **Improve the health and wellbeing** of over one billion people by 2020.
2. **Halve the environmental footprint** of Unilever's products by 2030.
3. **Enhance the livelihoods** of millions of people in the supply chain, particularly in developing countries.

By embedding sustainability into its business model, Unilever was not just aiming to comply with regulations – it was positioning itself as a leader in environmental and social responsibility, ensuring that the company would remain competitive in a rapidly changing world.

No palm oil and smarter packaging, please

Unilever's plan was built on several key pillars, each addressing a different aspect of sustainability. One of the most significant areas of focus was sustainable sourcing. The company committed to sourcing 100 per cent of its agricultural raw materials from sustainable sources by 2020. This included everything from tea and palm oil to soy and vegetables.

Palm oil, in particular, was a major focus. The production of palm oil is known to contribute to deforestation, habitat destruction and human rights violations. Unilever set aggressive targets to source only certified sustainable palm oil, which was a challenge, given the complexity of the supply chain. However, by working closely with suppliers and not-for-profits, the company made significant progress towards this goal.

Another important aspect of the plan was reducing waste and water usage in the production process. Unilever committed to cutting its water use in production and reducing the waste generated by its products, for example the company redesigned product packaging to use less plastic and reduce waste, while also promoting recycling efforts among consumers.

The outcome: a competitive edge and positive impact

The results of Unilever's 'what if' scenario planning were impressive. By 2020, the company had made significant strides toward its sustainability goals, for example Unilever achieved its target of sourcing 100 per cent of its tea for Lipton from Rainforest Alliance Certified farms. Additionally, the company has reduced its greenhouse gas emissions through the way it manufactures, packages and transports products by 65 per cent since 2008, showing a clear commitment to reducing its environmental impact.

Unilever's focus on sustainability also proved to be a competitive advantage. As consumers became more environmentally conscious, they increasingly chose brands that aligned with their values. Unilever brands like Ben & Jerry's, which emphasised fair trade practices and environmental stewardship, saw a surge in popularity. Similarly, the company's Dove brand, which promotes body positivity and social causes, gained loyal customers who appreciated its commitment to more than just profits.

Three long-range lessons
Unilever's success with its Sustainable Living Plan offers several key lessons for businesses:

- **The value of long-term thinking:** By running 'what if' scenarios about the future demand for sustainable practices, Unilever was able to prepare for a shifting global landscape. The company wasn't just reacting to changes – it was anticipating them.
- **The integration of sustainability and profitability:** Unilever proved that sustainability and profitability can go hand in hand. By reducing waste, using resources more efficiently, and aligning its products

with consumer values, Unilever demonstrated that doing good for the planet can also be good for business.

- **The power of collaboration for change:** Achieving large-scale sustainability goals required collaboration with various stakeholders, including suppliers, governments, not-for-profits and consumers. Unilever's commitment to sustainable sourcing, especially for raw materials like palm oil, showed the power of partnerships in driving change.

The 'what if' factor

Unilever's success in running 'what if' scenarios illustrates the transformative power of foresight and proactive action. By asking tough questions about the future of sustainability, the company not only prepared for a changing world but also became a leader in environmental stewardship. For businesses looking to stay competitive while making a positive impact, Unilever's journey offers a powerful roadmap for integrating sustainability into long-term strategy.

For each of us, running 'what if' scenarios is a powerful way to explore and test multiple versions of the future. Just like a pilot does in a simulator, running new scenarios enables us to imagine what might be possible, imagine how things could change and prepare for change by developing greater flexibility in our thinking.

> ### High-AQ habit: Run 'what if' scenarios
>
> This is a simple habit that encourages you to think about a range of scenarios and think through how you would adapt to them. Run them on your own, or gather your team and ask everyone to list as many scenarios as they can, then talk through how you would respond to each. For example, a company might ask:
>
> **What if** a major competitor launches a revolutionary new product?
> *Running this scenario could lead to strategies for innovation, market differentiation or customer loyalty initiatives that help the company stay competitive regardless of what the competitor does.*
>
> **What if** the power cut out to a major work site?
> *Running this scenario could lead to different decisions around the reliability of existing power sources and considerations for new sources.*
>
> **What if** Apple started selling the product that our business produces?
> *Running this scenario could generate an entirely new marketing approach that leads to building stronger ties with your customers and community.*
>
> **What if** a critical component of our manufacturing process was no longer available?

> *Running this scenario could lead directly to sourcing new and local suppliers, or figuring out how the operation could build in new business continuity measures.*

Asking 'what if' can tilt your thinking sideways. This simple provocation encourages creative and long-term thinking by challenging the status quo. It opens up the possibility of considering radical changes or innovations that could disrupt the current environment, helping to anticipate and potentially lead future trends.

If you pose this question in time, it may also one day save your business. In early 2020, I was running a workshop with a large business that sells hearing aids. It was a franchise, and most of the franchises were independently owned by sole traders around Australia, mostly families who had made a huge bet on a 'safe' game. The market for hearing aids is a well-established one and, with an aging population, one that is low risk.

The owners were asking me about connecting with clients in the local community, an increasing number of players coming into the market, and how to safeguard against Specsavers, who were now running hearing tests annually, when people popped back in to have their eye testing done so their prescription was current. These were early signals, each of them alarming. But there was one dangerous assumption here: that major disruption could not possibly come from an entirely different industry.

The four principles

Someone in the room posed this question: 'What if Apple started selling AirPods as hearing aids?' Exactly. The rumours were rife back in 2020, and this room needed to take that signal seriously. It made complete sense from Apple's position to enter the hearing care market, as they already had a strong market presence in audio and communications devices.

That single move could make traditional hearing aids potentially obsolete overnight. It would entirely reposition the stigma attached to wearing hearing aids and make them not just cool, but compulsory. It would engage people in understanding more about the role of hearing in staying socially connected and help people adapt to using aids when they need to, which is usually years before people are actually converted to buying them.

It stunned the room. Four years on, the rumours are stronger than ever about Apple entering the hearing aid market in 2025. And why wouldn't the tech giant add technology to devices that so many of us already use?

As of September 2024, a statement on Apple's website explains that Apple has collaborated with manufacturers to develop various hearing and accessibility technology, including hearing aids, cochlear implants and sound processors designed specifically for Apple devices. They add that that these hearing devices provide excellent sound quality, and offer many helpful features via Bluetooth, as many other devices do. They can also input presets from the user's audiologist to adapt to different environments.

Activate

Asking 'what if?' without any constraints has profound value, with the potential to affect the way we do business and the way we live our lives by reminding us of the simple fact that anything is possible.

6

Release

The fourth step to being in a continual conversation with change

It's difficult to be the author of your life script if you're rehearsing to be an extra in someone else's.

In the late 1990s, GoldCorp, a Canadian mining company, was on the brink of collapse. Its Red Lake mine in Ontario had exhausted its easily accessible gold and traditional methods of prospecting had failed to uncover new reserves. Rob McEwen, the CEO, was determined to find a solution. Rather than relying on the company's internal geologists, he decided to take an unconventional approach that would revolutionise the mining industry. McEwen had a bold idea: what if he could leverage the power of collective intelligence to find new gold deposits?

The four principles

In 2000, he launched the GoldCorp Challenge, a pioneering open-innovation initiative. He made an unprecedented move by releasing 50 years' worth of the company's geological data to the public. This was a radical departure from the norm, as such data was typically considered highly confidential in the mining industry. McEwen believed that by opening up the data, he could tap into a global pool of talent that could potentially find what his team could not – a not-so-small move that could change GoldCorp's long game.

The challenge offered a total prize of US$575,000 to participants who could identify the most promising drilling targets. The response was overwhelming. Over 1400 participants from more than 50 countries – including geologists, engineers and mathematicians – entered the competition. Many of these individuals had no prior experience in mining but brought fresh perspectives and innovative techniques to the table.

The results were transformative. The winning submissions not only identified 110 new targets but also pointed out locations that had been previously overlooked by GoldCorp's own team. The predictions turned out to be remarkably accurate. The new exploration led to the discovery of eight million ounces of gold, turning the Red Lake mine into one of the richest gold mines in the world.

This discovery catapulted GoldCorp from near bankruptcy to one of the most profitable mining companies globally. The success of the GoldCorp Challenge demonstrated the immense potential of open innovation. By inviting external experts to solve a problem traditionally handled in-house, McEwen was able to achieve breakthroughs that had eluded his team. The initiative also highlighted the value of cross-disciplinary collaboration, as many of the successful participants came from fields outside of mining, offering unique insights that GoldCorp's internal team lacked.

Beyond the immediate financial success, the GoldCorp Challenge had a lasting impact on the mining industry and the broader business community. It showed that opening up a company's challenges to external problem solvers could lead to innovative solutions, even in industries that had long relied on proprietary knowledge and internal expertise. The challenge became a case study in business schools and a model for how companies could harness the power of crowdsourcing and open innovation to drive growth and solve complex problems.

We run this case study with every leadership cohort to reinforce a powerful point: to consider what McEwan had to 'release'. His willingness to let go of ego, status and tradition to leverage brilliant minds across different industries not only saved his company but showed what is possible when we open our minds to the notion that 'what has got me here won't get me there'. How many top CEOs do you see making a move as bold as this to find their version of gold? It's an extraordinary story.

> ### Principle #4: Release
>
> Be an active player in change by releasing what you no longer need, to free up the energy and mind space you need for the new. Identify what beliefs, habits, skills, people or values are no longer fit for purpose or no longer aligned with where you are headed. Let go of what no longer serves you.
>
> **The high-AQ habits that support this principle are:**
> - embrace constructive destruction
> - scroll back to look forward
> - rethink your role models
> - run the five Ls.

High-AQ habit: Embrace constructive destruction

'Constructive destruction' sounds complex, but it's really very simple, and necessary when we're adopting a mindset and practices that allow us to effectively and efficiently adapt to change. Constructive destruction means that, in order to build something new and valuable, it may be necessary to dismantle or let go of what is no longer serving its purpose. This concept is closely related to the idea of 'creative destruction', famously introduced by economist Joseph Schumpeter, which describes how economic innovation leads to the demise of outdated industries and practices. However, 'constructive destruction' puts a more intentional and positive spin on the process, promoting destruction as a necessary and deliberate step in creating something better. Constructive destruction is another way to describe 'unlearning'. And the purpose is the same: to recognise and discard outdated habits, mindsets or processes in order to foster growth, adaptability and progress. It's about seeing the value in letting go of what no longer works to make room for new possibilities.

The ultimate act of unlearning: the backwards bicycle experiment

There is one specific and mind-bending experiment that lands this point in less than ten minutes. And it's because most of us know how to ride a bike. The way we do it is deeply embedded in our brain. Destin Sandlin, of the YouTube channel SmarterEveryDay, shows us exactly how our brains learn and unlearn tasks.

Sandlin worked with a group of engineers who one day decided to play a trick on him. They modified his bike so that turning the handlebars to the right made the front wheel turn left and vice versa. This simple change created a profound challenge for anyone trying to ride the bicycle, even for highly skilled cyclists. Sandlin attempted to ride the backwards bicycle and discovered that his brain, which had been trained to ride a normal bicycle since childhood, could not easily adapt to this new situation. He was obviously extremely frustrated by not being able to ride the bike even a few metres. (You can see this 2015 video for yourself, 'The backwards brain bicycle', on YouTube.)

Despite knowing consciously how the bicycle worked, his ingrained motor skills made it nearly impossible to ride the bike without extensive practice. After eight months of daily practice, something in his brain 'clicked', and he was able to ride the backwards bicycle successfully, showing how deeply ingrained the original skill had been, and how difficult it is to rewire the brain for a new version of the same task.

The remarkable human brain

One of the key lessons from the experiment involves the concept of neuroplasticity – the brain's ability to form and reorganise synaptic connections, especially in response to learning or experience. The experiment demonstrates that while the brain is incredibly adaptable, unlearning a deeply ingrained skill is much harder than learning a new one from scratch. This is because the neural pathways associated with the original skill are so well established that they dominate any new learning, requiring a significant and sustained effort to change. The experiment has broader implications beyond just riding a bicycle. It highlights how our habits and cognitive biases can be deeply entrenched, making change difficult even when we know it's necessary. This has applications in various fields such as education, behavioural change and even business practices, where unlearning outdated models or methods is crucial for innovation.

Children and unlearning

The second most stunning discovery in Sandlin's experiment was when his young son learnt to ride the backwards bicycle much faster than he could – in less than two weeks! It was a real-life example of how plastic a child's brain is. Children are less burdened by established neural pathways and so can adapt to new tasks more easily. It emphasises the importance of fostering adaptability and openness to new learning from a young age.

The experiment teaches us about the challenges of changing deeply ingrained habits and underscores the brain's remarkable but sometimes stubborn plasticity; the older we get, the more conscious we need to be about our unconscious dedication to the status quo.

> ### High-AQ habit: Embrace constructive destruction
>
> We may not have a team of engineers who can build a backwards bicycle for us, but we can still embrace unlearning by picking up something as simple as a pen. We can test our ability to 'unlearn' by learning to write with our opposite hand. This is a powerful exercise in rewiring your brain. It's so simple, but this practice challenges your established motor skills and forces your brain to adapt to new ways of thinking and moving. As you struggle to write with your non-dominant hand, you're essentially unlearning the ingrained habits of your dominant hand, breaking neural connections that have long been automatic. This process not only enhances your cognitive flexibility but also demonstrates how unlearning requires deliberate practice and patience. By embracing this challenge, you

train your brain to be more adaptable, opening the door to new ways of thinking and problem-solving.

Step 1: Writing with your dominant hand
Objective: To demonstrate automatic habits.
Action: Write the sentence 'I am learning to unlearn', using your dominant hand.
Reflection prompt: How did it feel to write this? Was the process automatic?

Step 2: Writing with your non-dominant hand
Objective: To experience the discomfort of unlearning.
Action: Write the same sentence with your non-dominant hand. Expect to find it slow and awkward!
Reflection prompt: How did writing with the other hand feel? What emotions came up? How frustrated were you? Be honest!

Step 3: Relate this experience to unlearning generally
Objective: To make the connection between this experience and the general experience of unlearning, because writing with the opposite hand parallels the process of unlearning in life.
Action: Think about where you need to unlearn habits, and reflect on how the exercise makes clear the patience and effort needed for change.
Reflection prompt: How does this experience relate to unlearning in other areas of your life?

High-AQ habit: Scroll back to look forward

How do we challenge and discard outdated habits, mindsets or processes to foster growth, adaptability and progress? How do we unlearn, or 'destroy', older ways of doing business to introduce new, more efficient or user-friendly approaches?

Here is one of my all-time favourite exercises to run with a group. 'Scrolling back to look forward' on our own personal timeline helps us understand how much change we are capable of and opens up our perspective on what's possible when we apply more intention to our future timeline.

High-AQ habit: Scroll back to look forward

1. **Scroll back**: Choose one social media platform you use, and scroll back ten years (if you can). What were you posting about back then? What was your first ever post on Instagram, Facebook or LinkedIn?
2. **Reflect on milestone events**: Think about significant events, decisions and trends that occurred during that period. Consider what led to these developments and how they shaped your present. What was your view of the world then? What were your values? What did you fundamentally believe to be true and 'unchangeable' about your world? What has, in fact, changed? Were you intentional about how the past ten years unfolded?

> 3. **Project forward:** Based on your discoveries, think about looking ten years ahead, with more intention. What might be possible for you in the future? Consider possible scenarios and their implications.
> 4. **Apply insights:** Use these insights to inform your current strategies, decisions and plans. Consider how understanding the past can help you navigate future uncertainties more effectively.

High-AQ habit: Rethink your role models

'ANDREA – YOUR SCRIPT IN THREE MINUTES!'

This unnecessarily blunt command silenced the newsroom. No warmth, no 'please', and definitely no concern for the fact that I hadn't eaten since I swiped in seven hours ago. I was on the kind of deadline that would send a surge of adrenaline blasting through the body of any journalist: scripting a story that was leading the midday news bulletin of an international broadcaster, with potential reach across the Middle East, Africa, Europe and Latin America – 200 million viewers. In a fifteen-year career in loud, chaotic (and incredibly fun) newsrooms, where unruly orders were the norm from top leadership, a condescending bark like this had never before caused me to physically halt. It was the first direction in my entire career that both hit, held down and forced me to control my anger management button, and I was suddenly allergic to how it made me feel.

I'd spent my professional life working with ultra-high-performance news crews where every day was an exceptional lesson in teamwork, and I had a long-standing track record of being a zero-drama, highly compliant team player who accepted that an occasional harsh tone from the production desk was part of the process. But in this moment, a valid question was raised: *Is this my definition of success?*

The person speaking to me held a coveted and commanding role in a high-stakes environment. I'd looked at him every day for the past year, but never with such clarity. Objectively, he was lacking basic traits that I associated with strong role models: humble, empathic, inspirational, motivating. I was staring at an anti-role model. This was an uncomfortable moment because, as I continued typing, I was slowly realising that I was on a narrow path to a future in which I was a person I didn't want to be. And it prompted a valid line of enquiry.

On the ten-block walk home past the White House, I started thinking back through other defining moments, when people around me had shown me the opposite of what I'd seen today. One rather dramatic story instantly surfaced, involving a person who hit it out of the park, even in the pitch-black hole of a blindingly stressful moment.

Fairly early on in my television career I found myself upside down in a helicopter cockpit, ditched in salt water. Disoriented and stunned, I knew that all I had to do was hit the release button on the seatbelt harness, but I could not connect my brain with my arms. My hands lay limp on either side of the double-locked buckle.

The four principles

The chopper had started to sink, but we had to stay put until the cabin stabilised. As we rolled through a genuinely disorienting 180-degree turn, I took a shallow breath and found myself struggling to send a signal from my brain to my hands to simply release the restraint, so I could open the door and swim to the surface. It should have been as instinctive as picking up a cup of coffee, but I suspect a degree of shock had set in.

This experience was part of a structured emergency training exercise that certified me to fly in the network helicopter, but even so, for me it was going very wrong. I was in the front left-hand side of the chopper, with a very capable Air Force pilot seated to my right and three rescue divers on the margins.

I was beyond even asking for help. The pilot could see what was happening. He exited the craft, then turned back around, snapped the latch of my harness, grabbed my right arm and dragged me out and up. It probably took two seconds, but it seemed to play out in slow motion. Our briefing had been clear: it was every person for themselves. The entire point of such an intense drill was to be tested, to be stressed to the absolute max, and to survive using your own individual awareness. This wasn't an exercise in team-building or helping others; it was purely to build individual skill.

In the moment, I didn't think much about what that pilot did for me, but as I reflected, the lesson sharpened up. He could easily have left me there and let the rescue divers do their thing. Instead, he ignored the rules of the game and showed off some best-practice role-modelling. There's a metaphor somewhere in there for real leadership on a more prosaic level: a person sharp enough to scan vast, chaotic, dynamic and often crisis-stricken environments while remaining forensically connected to what is unfolding right beside them.

Until my near-drowning incident, I had always been slightly confused about what constituted good leadership. I was surrounded by adults who were more important than me in the standard hierarchical sense, but only a few offered motivation, inspiration or guidance. I wanted more for myself, so I moved to Washington, DC, in my late twenties with no job, no money and nothing resembling a sensible plan. It was a massive gamble on my own growth, which was the point. I was in the market for role models who I could look up to and learn from. And what a pay-off. Seven years of working in and around the White House, State Department and Pentagon exposed me to extraordinary levels of vision and human capability. I routinely interviewed people who woke up every day to serve the nation or the community in ways that left me without words. I spoke with families of 9/11 victims; soldiers undergoing rehabilitation at Walter Reed Army Medical Center; scientists at NASA; the former director of the Federal Emergency Management Agency (FEMA), James Lee Witt; and the first woman to be appointed chief scientist of the US National Oceanic and Atmospheric Administration (NOAA), Sylvia Earle, to name a few. They were life-changing conversations with the real deal makers and policy challengers.

What makes a good role model?

There's a quality that these minds, and my personal rescue pilot, have in common: they are each someone we can look up to and learn from. As expert on trust Rachel Botsman explains so masterfully in her November 2023 'Rethink' newsletter, strong role models serve three distinct functions:

1. They inspire us by showing us what is possible.
2. They influence goals and motivation.
3. They serve as a behavioural example of success.

'Role models should not be based on power, fame and influence,' Botsman explains. 'They need to be reclaimed from images of perfectionism that are feeding unhealthy perceptions of achievement and success. It would be wonderful if we were raising kids who could name more nurses, teachers or community workers as role models than celebrities or social media influencers. Good role models should not solely be based on *what people do* (and how successful they are) but on why they do it.'

Paying attention to signals of change is the starting point for exercising a higher degree of personal agency over our future. And when the signal of change is a person, we need to acknowledge what it means and decide how we're going to respond. While I was writing my script that day, I still had the mental flexibility to run my life through a few alternate future scenarios in my head – and they all ended up in the same place. I decided that day that my television career was over. My newsroom boss – a very senior international producer – will never know, but he was a conductor for the best decision I've ever made.

Two weeks later, I swiped out for the last time, and as I dropped my security pass behind the desk at reception, I said an audible 'Thank you!' for the gift of the anti-role model. An anti-role model can serve as a valuable signpost; can help us assess whether we're in the right place, on the right path and around people who prompt us to imagine what's *truly* possible for ourselves. It was time to change the course coordinates for a new shoreline. I was the author of this new script, and I was perfectly at ease with it being a blank screen.

Anti-role models create a stronger axis of values

'Having an anti-role model is in many ways a stronger values compass than a role model,' says Botsman. 'An anti-role model is a way of looking at someone else's choices and behaviours and saying, "I don't want to be anything like that!" It's something to push against. Think Lance Armstrong, Bernie Madoff, Elon Musk or Sam Bankman-Fried.'

You don't feel aligned with the anti-role model's intentions, behaviour or ethics. You don't see them demonstrating respect, humility, integrity or empathy. You're uncomfortable with how they use their power, money or success. Or perhaps they simply don't make you feel good about yourself.

Rethinking role models comes down to our definition of success, says Botsman. 'While role models can feed into fairy-tales, anti-role models can serve as cautionary tales.'

The four principles

A checklist for the right role model
1. Am I aligned with the way my current role model demonstrates their values, intentions and behaviours?
2. Am I consistently inspired and encouraged to pursue my dreams?
3. Do they represent a future version of myself?

High-AQ habit: Run the five Ls
The ultimate New Year's resolution

Maybe it's a sign that I'm getting older, but I'm finding myself developing an allergy to New Year's resolutions – they're just so 1992, the cassette tape of early January habits.

At the end of last year, I found myself making a list for the year ahead that included all the usual suspects: lose the last four Covid kilograms, work smarter, get up earlier, walk 5000 steps every day, etc., etc. It was undeniably underwhelming. I might as well have just dug out my scratchpad from the end of 2021, 2022 and 2023, because it'd look exactly the same, word for word. Just a laundry list of micro fails on repeat.

Searching for an upgrade, I started scanning my office for souvenirs of the year. Apparently, I had scribbled my way through 400 virtual meetings using ten yellow A4 Spirax notebooks. And halfway through notebook three, I found *exactly* what I needed. It was the rough note-taking from a confronting, introspective exercise that I heard Dominic Price share with a crowd earlier in the year which is far more powerful than any rehashed list of resolutions. Price is a work futurist at Atlassian, and he calls this exercise 'The Five Ls'. It's a simple set of questions designed to help you reflect on upping your overall leadership and life game. It's about going *all-in* on improving yourself.

What I love most about the five Ls is that it's a discovery tour of yourself – your habits, behaviours and ecosystem. Done properly, it's a deeply worthy conversation that inevitably raises questions around what you need to let go of in order to energise yourself for what's next; what you need to dial down and dial up; what you need to release.

Think of it as a long, hard look in the mirror with fluorescent lighting and absolutely no filters available to you. Price is clear that this is about *you* being the best version of yourself. I completely endorse his thinking – if we don't routinely assess what drives us or holds us back, how can we lead ourselves or anyone else with any degree of impact, whether in our workplace, family or community?

So if you're all-in on some self-discovery, I suggest finding a colleague or friend who has no filter. I'm finding that *this* is the magic part of the mix – that person who supports you, but doesn't let you get away with anything. I hit up my genius friend Alicia Stephenson (aka Stevie) and the result was that the five Ls kicked off a two-day creative strategy work bender that led to an entirely fresh vision for 2024 (which included this book). So thank you, Dom and Stevie.

High-AQ habit: Run the five Ls

The five Ls will take less than an hour, and it goes something like this:

Step 1. Create seven columns labelled: Milestones, LOVED, LOATHED, LONGED FOR, LEARNED, LAUGH AT and Actions. Before the session, agree on the time period you'd like to look back on. In my case it was twelve months, but we're committed to doing it every 90 days in the future.

Note: if you're running this on the phone or (trigger warning) MS Teams call, then agree on a collaboration doc (Trello, Monday, Asana, even a Word doc in Google Drive, etc.). For in-person teams, find a whiteboard or large sheet of paper and set out sticky notes and markers – because who doesn't love a disproportionate use of sticky notes?

2. Set the stage
We're here to explore how to improve, not to recycle our misplaced imposter syndrome or dwell on the negatives. Let's stay positive and focused.

3. Milestones
OK, let's talk about the key events that happened. What were your milestones, goals met, highlights? And how did you feel about them?

4. Reflect

Use the five Ls as prompts for reflection, and note your responses in the relevant column:

LOVED: What you loved about your work; how you led over the time period.

This is what you want to keep doing, or do more of, in the future. What can you double-down on?

LONGED FOR: What you wish you'd had.

This could be more real-life events, more exercise, more coffee (no judgement here!).

LOATHED: What made life harder? What was deeply irritating? What do you hope will never happen again?

LEARNED: What have you learned from your successes and your mistakes?

LAUGH AT: What has made you belly laugh?

If we're not having fun, what's the point, right?

5. Actions

Let's talk about:

- One action you'll take to remove something from your LOATHED list.
- One action you'll take to amplify something from your LOVED list.

The four principles

- Using your LONGED FOR, LEARNED and LAUGH AT lists to help shape your ideas for what actions to take.

6. Close it out and schedule the next five Ls meet-up.

How did the five Ls play out for you? Any revelations, discoveries or breakthroughs?

For me, it's a high-fidelity example of what having a high AQ is all about – letting go of old beliefs, ideas and rituals that are no longer 'fit for purpose' so we can free up our headspace for more modern ways of living and working that support where we're headed. Part of moving towards our favourite kind of future is understanding what's changing around us – and being decisive about what's coming with us, and what we're leaving behind (farewell, conventional list of New Year's resolutions).

The five Ls is still a set of intentions, but it's one that helps us think differently. It's simple, structured, meaningful and gives us clear direction. It's helped me reflect far more deeply on my habits, mindset, skillset and priorities. In fact, it was the catalyst for me recalling my all-time favourite subject at school – creative writing. How could I connect back with the love of that and unapologetically do more of it? Well, start a work/life newsletter, and just start writing. Then follow it up with a new book.

Undeniably, the true benefit of the five Ls is running it on the regular with someone who will call you out on your bullshit, keep you honest, amplify and support you – because rarely can we grow or make significant shifts in isolation. It was a no-brainer for Stevie and me to commit to meeting every quarter, with strict guidelines to set the stage for genuine and sustained growth – we need to be in-person, on a lounge, by a pool, under an umbrella, without dogs or kids.

Maybe you can join us, and we can all figure out what we need to release to make way for what's next.

Part 3

What's next?

7

The energy for change

It took a dramatic fainting incident for Dr Simone Scovell, a leading healthcare pioneer in Australia and close friend of mine, to realise that something was very wrong with her life. She learnt about the importance of energy management the hard way.

At the age of 29, Simone was working as a senior resident in cardiothoracic surgery at one of the country's best hospitals – until one day she passed out in the operating theatre, mid-surgery, and woke up to a sliced face and broken nose from the fall.

Scovell was working 115-hour weeks, including a lot of on-call work at whatever hour of the night a heart became available for a transplant. Her dedication to work was absolute, and as she reflects honestly, like many overachievers, she enjoyed the constant adrenaline of what she was doing. Scovell was deeply committed to helping people; as a teenager she'd made the decision to become a doctor as she witnessed her mum's ordeal with uterine cancer, and the toll it took on her dad.

Despite a full schedule representing Australia in basketball while studying medicine, she realised her dream. But the faultline in her non-stop lifestyle had begun to crack open.

Reflecting back to that day in the operating theatre, Scovell had known something wasn't right as soon as she'd woken up that morning, but ignored her instincts. She hadn't slept in days and could barely move. She recalls:

> I called my senior surgeon to let him know I wasn't feeling good. Against my better judgement, guilt took over and I ended up at work. In the second surgery of the day, I collapsed. On the way down, I collected the corner of a surgical tray, which sliced my face in half and broke my nose. I also smashed my hope of being top of my field. As a patient in my own workplace, and while still in the hospital bed, I resigned from my position and vowed to make a change not only for myself, but to help change the way organisations look after their people.

The 29-year-old decided to prioritise her own health, and also began forming in her mind the embryonic stages of the global healthcare business she later founded, TOTIUM.

Scovell's 115-hour weeks had been fuelled by coffee, adrenaline and the ability to override all the signals her body was sending her. She is still a chronic overachiever: she holds three degrees and is currently completing a fourth, an Associate Degree in Artificial Intelligence in Healthcare at Stanford University's School of Medicine. She runs a global business and sits on advisory boards. All this in addition to her most important role – being a mum.

But her priorities have firmly shifted: her health comes first, and her other commitments fit around that. She knows she can't be a good mum, family member or business leader without taking care of herself.

The energy for change

Many of us have a version of Scovell's story. While this example might sound extreme, I'm frequently hearing of people who have, quite literally, hit the wall. And in the current landscape of constant change, learning to manage our own energy and intervene long before the brutal smack of burnout hits is one of the most important things we can do for ourselves.

I'd like you to think back to Chapter 2, 'Modern success metrics'. Where did you place yourself and your own health when you were thinking about your version of success? If you didn't prioritise health, I want you to revisit the chapter. Because being an active participant in shaping change requires significant energy – mental, physical, emotional and spiritual. Trust me, I know. Let me share the story of my own wake-up call.

What's next?

When the sanctuary becomes the situation room

It was early 2010 and I was working as a reporter on Capitol Hill in Washington, DC. I'd just made the six-hour trip to Los Angeles, my first work trip for the year. I was staying in room 803, the same room at the same hotel I always stayed in for my weekly trips to LA. There was a strong sense of familiarity and 'home away from home'.

But it turned out to be a later check-in than I had planned, after 10 pm on a Saturday night, when there was one person on reception and a lobby filled with very trendy Los Angeles people talking about their start-ups. I pushed myself into the elevator and stepped off on level eight while the rest of the group went straight to the rooftop bar – the night was only just starting for them.

The door to my room felt heavier than usual, a sign of the fatigue kicking in after the six-hour flight and the additional six hours of packing, transfers, check-ins and delays. But as I stepped through the doorway and firmly parked my suitcase against the wall, I felt something that was clearly more than the usual feeling of fatigue. Having worked in war zones and disaster zones across the globe and travelled extensively for years, I was familiar with exhaustion. This was something different.

It was as though my mind had been hijacked. My heart started to pound and I felt a wave of fear, a crushing, isolating darkness, consuming me. It felt like I was having a heart attack. I actually thought I was dying. I opened the door, sat down in the hallway with my phone and pressed 9-1-1. But I paused before

The energy for change

I pressed CALL. Only because I'd been through it twice before did I know what was happening to me in this moment: I was having a full-blown anxiety attack. I somehow stopped the debilitating spiral by taking very deep breaths to slow the descent into chaos, and stabilise my system.

The sanctuary of room 803 became the situation room. It was triggering my system into meltdown. Neither my body nor my brain were coping with the thought of facing another year of such a punishing schedule, a schedule that included 100 flights a year. They were screaming out to stop everything and get off this wild ride.

The crushing feeling I felt was a signal of change I could not ignore. I called a close friend who was a surgeon and simply said, 'I'm pretty sure I need your help.'

The harshest of reality checks

Perhaps to everyone around me, my life looked pretty good. And it really was. I was a television news reporter and producer, freelancing for several major outlets. It was my dream gig in a city that I had dreamed of living in since a family holiday in 1987. I was living in the centre of the news universe, covering the major US breaking stories that set the daily agenda around the Pentagon, State Department and White House. I had landed in Tbilisi, Georgia as Russian tanks rolled out; woken up to car bombs in Baghdad; bailed up Brad Pitt at the opening of *Babel*; and after hours, when I was at home in Washington, I'd unwind by hanging over the fence to talk all things aviation with my favourite neighbour, who happened to be a former US Air Force pilot and NASA liaison to the Department of Homeland Security.

I loved every day of it.

But the reality was, I was a complete train wreck. Fifteen-hour days meant eating on the go and no time to work out. Days turned into months and months turned into six years of neglecting the basics. I'd take an Ambien to get to sleep and several Nurofen when I woke up, after hitting the snooze button as many times as I could get away with. I stacked on 20 kilograms and blanked on my best friend's birthday, year after year. I got angry over small interactions and frequently had to stop myself from escalating situations. I was late to everything. I found myself crying on the bathroom floor, and on overnight flights back to Washington. I'd signed up to this entire system and was holding on to it tightly. If I couldn't cope, I thought, there must be something wrong with *me*.

The signals became louder: I smashed my left elbow falling out of a bar and onto a street. Even a US$30,000 surgery and two years of excruciating rehab (which cost another US$30,000) didn't prompt any realisation that radical change was required. Looking at my diary around that time gave me anxiety. Every day was overscheduled, for 60 days in a row. I was collecting red flags on a road to burnout, and I ignored them all. The lies we tell ourselves, right?

Then I checked into room 803. And I face-planted into a significant health event that could take me down in one fell swoop if I looked the other way, rather than facing the multiple slingshots of signals fired my way. I've been on a mission to help other people avoid this same fall ever since.

Four steps to self-management

The morning after my episode, I silently processed the advice from my surgeon friend, and came to a conclusion so powerful it formed the key steps of this book. I needed to confront four things:

- **Engage** in the signals of change.
- **Accept** that this lifestyle was not working.
- **Activate** my optimism for new possibilities and make a one-year plan to change that would lead to a huge pay-off in ten years.
- **Release** any degree of 'status' that was loosely attached to my job.

My application of the four steps was as extreme as the incident itself. Essentially, I put my life in a shredder and set it on fire. I had to admit that this period was over, bid farewell to my amazing US network, and walk away from my career. I had to pack my life up, move back to Melbourne, Australia, and start from scratch. I prioritised my wellbeing and began to rebuild myself from the inside out. I knew that it was going to be a tough few years. It turns out that was a wild understatement – it was a thousand times harder than I'd imagined. But looking back now, the pay-off from that decision was profound.

What's next?

I could only be the happiest version of myself today – personally, professionally, emotionally – because of the episode in room 803.

As we've covered in this book, I am a fan of 'small moves' that we can make to change the longer game, or trying out what we can ramp up and dial down as mini-experiments to see what we can shift without overinvesting. But in this particular case, I knew there was no way I could dial down my shifts, or dial up my boundaries. There's little margin for negotiating in a newsroom or the lifestyle it requires, so I knew it was either all in or all out.

Energy awareness: a foundation for self-management

Only now can I recognise the signs of adrenal burnout that I missed back then, and understand how to manage, place and protect my energy. The popular saying is that 'Energy flows where attention goes', and if we're not intentional about our attention, our energy will flow in one direction – out into the tsunami of distractions we face every day.

This simple image, which I call the *energy curve*, is an updated version of the Yerkes-Dodson law, which is a model of the relationship between pressure and performance. It proposes that our performance increases with stress, but only to a point. Too little or too much stress results in a performance deficit.

I'd like you to think right now about where you currently sit on the energy curve.

The energy for change

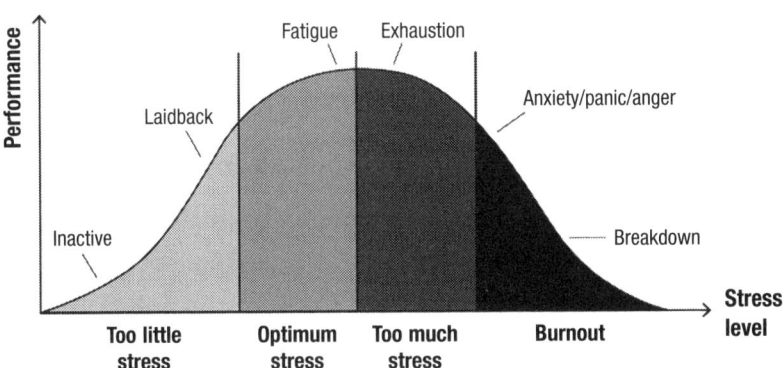

SOURCE: ANDREA CLARKE

How about at a time when you were at your best, or at your lowest?

I urge you to think carefully about precisely how much stress you need to be in a state of peak performance. And what specific indicators reveal that you're pushing over the line into the next zone.

Every time I run a masterclass, I ask the cohort which colour zone they're currently in and the response is usually very concerning. If you're in the third zone, tipping into the burnout zone, then you need to intervene. Stop what you're doing and go see your doctor.

Why is this so important now?

If we can't look after ourselves, we can't look after anyone else. As my executive coach and friend Lisa Stephenson, who I've quoted throughout this book, says, we're collectively exhausted. There's more change coming, and so many of us don't have the energy required to help shape our role in it.

What's next?

We're running on diminished reserves, looking for ways to energise ourselves and find inspiration, and yet despite having access to more information than at any other time in history, we can't find the answers.

But that's part of the problem: we're consuming so much information we can't find our way through the maze. Astoundingly, our brains can unconsciously process around *11 million pieces of information per second*. Contrast this to conscious processing, which sits at around 40 to 50 bits per second – still very impressive numbers. But according to a 2020 study by multiple authors, including Professor Nilli Lavie from the University College of London's School of Psychology and Language Sciences, our brains have an upper limit on how much they can process at once, due to the constant but limited energy supply. If we've already checked emails, Instagram and LinkedIn, read the news, spoken with family, made school lunches, helped with some last-minute homework and negotiated traffic or public transport before 9 am, we've taken up a significant amount of our day's brain capacity by the time we're in the first meeting of the day. Certainly a lot more than we might have fifteen years ago.

Which is why we need to know how to place and protect our energy, so that we can continue to lead ourselves and others effectively through change while having reserves for the unexpected.

The scientific concept of entropy is essentially the measure of disorder in a system, and the law of entropy finds that things fall into chaos if directed effort is not made to prevent it. It's the same with our energy: if we don't play an active role in directing it, entropy will take over. In my experience, the longer we leave situations without conscious attention, the more disruptive they become. When it comes to our energy, we must listen to the signals and take action early. We must be intentional, and constantly check in with ourselves to see where we're at on the curve, and where we need to tweak things. Importantly, if we're currently stuck in a cycle of survival (or the waiting place, which we explored in Chapter 4) due to a big project, life event or something we 'just have to get through', we absolutely must make sure there's an end date that we can focus on. For those of us who've spent years overriding our bodies' signals, there's a fine line between resilience and burnout.

The ideal performance equation

So where do we start? If we're to manage, place and protect our energy for high performance, then we need to understand the basics, such as where our energy comes from and how we protect it. In their 2003 book, *The Power of Full Engagement,* Dr Jim Loehr and Tony Schwartz offer up four dimensions of energy and a clear message: if any of these elements are over-stressed or under-stressed, our performance suffers.

The four elements
The four elements of the energy equation can be summarised as:
1. **Physical energy (quantity)**
   This refers to the amount of physical energy available.
   This is about the importance of maintaining physical

health through regular exercise, proper nutrition, adequate sleep and rest. Our physical wellbeing is the foundation for sustained energy levels and overall performance, and managing this principle effectively means you have enough energy.

2. **Emotional energy (quality)**
   This is about the nature of your emotional energy, which can range from positive emotions like joy and enthusiasm to negative ones like stress and frustration. Managing emotional energy involves actively cultivating positive emotions and managing negative ones. This can include developing emotional intelligence, practising gratitude, fostering positive relationships and engaging in activities that bring joy and satisfaction.

3. **Mental energy (focus)**
   This is about maximising your ability to concentrate on specific tasks and maintaining attention on what's important, with clarity and sharpness. It involves managing cognitive load, setting priorities, avoiding multitasking, taking regular breaks and engaging in activities that stimulate the mind and encourage creativity.

4. **Spiritual energy (force)**
   Your force is the passion and commitment with which you pursue your purpose and live according to your values. Spiritual energy is about connecting with your sense of purpose and meaning in life. It includes

The energy for change

deliberately aligning your actions with your core values, engaging in activities that fulfil you on a deeper level, and often involves practices such as meditation, mindfulness or connecting with a larger purpose or mission.

Loehr and Schwartz believe that the ideal equation is:

*Sustained performance = greatest **quantity** of energy + highest **quality** energy + clearest **focus** + maximum **force**.*

Maximising our energy quantity, quality, focus and force requires deliberate and active management. Understanding and managing these aspects can help you capture and sustain energy effectively across all dimensions of life, leading to better performance and wellbeing, and increased fulfilment. We usually feel like the best version of ourselves when we strike the right balance.

If you're stuck in a cycle that's draining your energy and this all feels overwhelming, the most powerful thing you can do is break it down and *do one thing.*

Like playing with small moves in a long game, coach Lisa Stephenson highlights the importance of simply starting with something, *anything*, to help shift your energy. Allocate fifteen minutes each day – or five, if that's all you can manage – to doing something new that feels good. Ask yourself right now: if you placed no limits on what you did in these fifteen minutes, who would you ring? What would you read? Where would you walk? Start there. When I was recovering from my own borderline adrenal burnout, I had a goal to walk 10,000 steps a day. It seemed utterly overwhelming – so I started with 1000 steps. Over a few months, I worked my way up to 10,000 steps and then it suddenly became the norm. I had to remind myself that it wasn't a race. As long I started moving in the right direction, the distance didn't matter. I wanted to build a way of living that I could sustain, especially through phases of relentless travel. Wherever I was going, I could always pack my sneakers and walk.

Optimising our energy

Sometimes when I work with clients or speak with executives, they're running on empty but say they're feeling great: they're excelling at work, running on four hours of sleep per night, enjoying a great, active social life, and still managing to exercise. I've been there too – sometimes I suspect it's the golden haze before the crash. In my experience, and based on everything I've learned from the medical and wellness experts that helped me get my life back on track, this golden haze is usually fuelled by adrenaline, which will, at some point, run out.

We all have different capacities when it comes to energy, stress and the impacts of adrenaline. I'm sure you've met someone who genuinely needs less sleep than the average person and seems to fit more into their days. There are also people who can run on adrenaline for years, but I'm yet to see anyone with a punishing lifestyle thrive long term. Inevitably, cracks begin to show. Energy awareness is a critical step in self-management, and without effective self-management we cannot lead others at the highest level. You must know yourself, your own triggers, and see the little signs that cracks are forming, and make small changes while it's still within your control, rather than waiting until the only option is to set your life on fire – aka me, circa 2010.

Optimising your energy in four simple steps

Based on research, trial, error, practice and work with thousands of clients, I've come up with four steps to help you optimise your energy:

1. **Draw on the four separate but related sources of energy**: This relates back to the four elements of energy we looked at above. Make sure you're addressing your requirements for physical, mental, emotional and spiritual energy.
2. **Balance energy spend with the required energy renewal**: This is simple mathematics. Sleep enough, eat enough nourishing food, hydrate, and maybe read a novel instead of a non-fiction book when your brain's had a big day. Where possible, reduce cognitive load by simplifying decisions and your life.
3. **Build capacity by pushing beyond our limits**: This one is often either overlooked or pushed to the extreme. Similar to the peak performance spot on the energy curve, there's mountains of evidence showing that we perform best when tasks are at a certain

level of difficulty. James Clear, author of the 2018 global bestseller *Atomic Habits*, says that the human brain loves a challenge, because your focus narrows, distractions fade away, and you find yourself fully invested in the task at hand. But the task needs to be within an optimal zone of difficulty. Clear refers to the Goldilocks Rule, which argues that motivation falters when challenges are too hard or too easy. Instead, our motivation reaches a peak when we're right at the edge of our capabilities.

Pushing just a little outside our comfort zone helps us increase our capacity. If you've ever lifted weights,

Physical (quantity)	Going to the gym three times a week – but no more	Getting a minimum of seven hours sleep per night, and a few extra hours on weekends
Emotional (quality)	Making sure you connect with at least three people you care about every day	Calling a friend for no specific reason – just to chat – at least once a week
Mental (focus)	Taking brain breaks at least twice a day: going for a quick walk, going to a different café for a change, doing a quick breathing exercise	Implementing strategies to reduce cognitive load: e.g. curating a 'work wardrobe' to reduce decision making, implementing a weekly routine for the non-negotiables
Spiritual (force)	Including feel-good activities that demand presence: e.g. walking along the beach every evening, taking an art class, getting lost in building sandcastles with your kids	Meditating for ten minutes a day

this is like an overload set where you push yourself beyond your limit, with support, for a brief spurt, in order to stimulate new muscle growth. The short-term pain leads to long-term gain, but if you overload too often you experience the opposite effect.

4. **Create positive energy rituals**: this is all about knowing what it is that fills your four buckets of physical, mental, emotional and spiritual energy, and creating rituals that help do this. Beyond the basics of sleep, nutrition and rest, this is about knowing yourself and what makes you feel good. Some examples of what this could look like include:

Walking every day	Cooking at home five times a week
Setting aside twenty minutes every day to spend *intentionally* with your family, pet, or a loved one	A daily emotional check-in with yourself, reflecting truthfully about how you're feeling
Reading a novel at night instead of more screen time	Swimming twice a week
Attending faith-based ceremonies	Conducting a monthly values audit to ensure you're living in alignment

Energy rituals don't have to make sense to anyone else. These are deeply personal, and can change to suit different stages of your life. There's no right or wrong here – it's about what works for you.

Learning from the best: what would an elite athlete do?

I have long been fascinated by high achievers from various fields, particularly elite athletes. A conversation with triple Olympian, Olympic bronze medallist and former captain of the Australian Stingers water polo team Rowie Webster gave me some fascinating insights into energy management.

Elite athletes are, in a way, taught how to override the signals their bodies send: an essential skill if you wake up feeling slightly off on the day of an Olympic final, and also important when training sessions demand you push through the barriers of pain in order to make incremental strength and fitness improvements when you're already so close to your peak. But they're also taught how to manage their reserves to make sure that on those big days, they have the best chance of waking up ready to perform at their best – and the mindset to show up at 100 per cent even when they're not feeling 100 per cent.

There are some practices in elite sport that help manage energy, many of which we can transfer to life and work: a coach who knows the limits of their athletes and applies individual management approaches, where appropriate, to maximise individual performance; a good team manager who clearly communicates where athletes need to be, when meals will be served and when there's time off, to minimise decision fatigue; and a team of physiotherapists, strength trainers and massage therapists to help athletes recover. But there are layers that Webster learned as she progressed through her career and became a master of self-management and, through her leadership journey from vice-captain to captain, a master of helping others manage their energy for peak performance.

There were some critical moments when Webster was called on to step up in all four of the energy domains – physical, mental, emotional and spiritual – and which taught her some valuable, lifelong lessons about the importance of energy management in leadership and change.

Webster was named captain of the Aussie Stingers in 2017, following the Rio Olympic Games and in the lead-up to the 2020 Tokyo Olympics (which were, of course, held in 2021 due to the global pandemic). Captaining the team through this period required an approach like no other: team members were dispersed in their home cities across Australia, with different athletes living in different conditions. For the Perth and Brisbane girls, it was largely business as usual when it came to training. For Webster, the only athlete based in Melbourne, access to gyms and pools was restricted for extended periods. She was lifting weights in the garage and swimming in the 11 degree Celsius waters of Port Phillip Bay throughout winter.

Her leadership and the team's modus operandi during this period was based on something she termed 'Project Human':

focusing much more on the person than the athlete. Her teammates were dealing with isolation, changes in work or university circumstances, lack of access to training and support staff, and missing family in different ways. Webster had to trust that her team members were training as best they could given the circumstances, and focus her energy on helping them manage their mental, emotional and spiritual energy. She had to hold the team together, and keep them focused on the goal of performing to medal standard at the Tokyo Olympic Games – even though, for much of this period, they didn't actually know when those games would be.

This period ended up preparing Webster for one of the most challenging moments in her life as an athlete and leader. The Stingers were at the Tokyo Olympics, and by all standards they had set for themselves they'd underperformed. They had missed the final four playoffs for a shot at the medals; an unfortunate one-goal loss to Russia in a goal-for-goal quarter-final match had relegated them to the playoffs for positions five to eight. Combined with the challenging eighteen-month lead-up to the Games, the loss had broken their hearts, confused their minds and drained every last drop of energy: physical, mental, emotional and spiritual. The team was spent, individually and collectively.

But there were two more matches to go.

'We had a choice,' reflects Webster. 'We could hang up our togs and just play out the remaining two games to finalise the placings, or we could do what Aussies do best and step up, bring our best, and give ourselves a red-hot go at finishing in

The energy for change

fifth place – the best we could do in the circumstances we were in – and hold our heads high. But how do you rally a team where everyone is in their own depth of despair, trying to process not only the loss and underperformance in the moment, but the trauma of the past eighteen months? The unfairness of entering an Olympic Games without a single international match as part of your preparation? How do you show up when your heart is broken?

'These were the questions I pondered as I tried to establish the path forward. It felt like there was nothing right to say, but a million wrong things. How do you unite people when they're all going through different stages of grief, anger and hurt? How do you avoid the temptation to blame? How do you find the connection point and pull people back together? How do you step up as a leader after so many mistakes have been made?

'I knew that this moment had nothing to do with physical energy, capability or skills. We *had* the capability and skills, and I know that if you take care of the mental and emotional energy, you can muster the physical. It's about mindset.

'After allowing some time to process and grieve, I ended up gathering the team together and asking my teammates a question: "In your mind, go back to the moment you first dreamed of representing Australia. If you could go back in time and ask that young girl to cap up and play for Australia once more at the Olympic Games, what would the answer be?"

'We all knew that winning our next two games to finish in fifth position rather than sixth, seventh or eighth didn't mean much to the average Aussie supporter. But finishing the tournament with pride and doing our absolute best for ourselves, our family and closest supporters meant more than we could articulate. Showing up when your heart is broken is one of the hardest things we can ask of ourselves. But after about five minutes of extreme emotional reflection, we all looked forward – I knew in that moment that there was a tacit agreement in the room. We focused on what we could control; we moved on and got ourselves ready faster than our opponents. After this moment, the energy started to return – in all its forms. I knew we were unbreakable. Our "comeback" to fifth place – while still laced with pain – is one of my proudest moments as an athlete and a leader.'

These days, having transitioned out of being an elite athlete into the world of coaching and representing other athletes on the Australian Olympic Committee's Athletes' Commission, Webster's approach to energy management is still a critical piece of her self-management and performance puzzle.

'When you learn to push beyond your limits as an athlete, there's safeguards in place to manage the impact – coaches, support teams and the like. When you're out on your own, it's tempting to keep pushing yourself. But it's not sustainable.'

Many high achievers I know can relate to this – we tell ourselves that we can live off four hours' sleep a night; that we can keep pushing; that we need to do it all. But like our brain capacity, our energy reserves are limited – and as Scovell's and my stories of burnout illustrate, if we don't take control when the signals start showing up, our bodies will force us to.

Webster's advice these days?

'Find one thing that nourishes you, and prioritise it. Protect that practice, whatever it is. For me, it's walking my dog Pickles at the park or the beach at the end of the day. It's where I process the day – I mentally file and consolidate what I've taken in, I check in with myself emotionally, and it's also a sort of spiritual reflection time. It's the most energising thing in my schedule, and it takes priority over almost everything else. I haven't yet found a way to get enough sleep in from Monday to Friday, but I know that as long as I have my time with Pickles, I'm OK.'

Webster's insights and practices translate beautifully to personal and workplace situations. And her Tokyo experience demonstrates the incredible power of focusing on the human when we lead ourselves and others through crises or intense challenges, and how critical our mindset is in managing and generating energy.

Your mindset is your most powerful tool

When we change the way we look at things, things start to shift around us. I talked about the power of reframing setbacks in Chapter 4, 'Accept', and Webster's story is a reminder of this important shift we have at our disposal: power over our own mindsets. As Webster reflected on her experience after the devastating loss at the Tokyo Olympics, the intentional change in mindset away from heartbreak towards the things that her teammates could control, and connecting them back to their *why*, helped shift them into gear and rebuild their energy.

What's next?

There's always something we can do to support our energy, and usually there's a cascade effect when we take positive action. Doing one thing from your 'rituals bucket' usually has a positive influence on all four types of energy. For example, I know that if I go for a walk along the beach, I physically feel better, my mind feels clearer, I feel more connected to who I am, and I also feel happier.

There is more within your control than you think. Sometimes, though, it will require some uncomfortable decisions.

Taking action

The intention of this chapter was threefold: to help you understand that change requires energy; to help you become more aware of your own energy as a tool for self-management; and to help you begin to implement some strategies to optimise your energy for performance and success according to *your* definition of it.

If you haven't found the place to start, try these steps – they're simple enough to do right now.

> **Energy curve check-in:** Where are you *today* on the energy curve? Think back to when too little or too much stress impacted your performance and wellbeing. What were some of the contributing factors, and how were you managing your energy (or not!) at that time?
>
> **Your energy equation check-in:** Apply the energy equation to yourself: how would you optimise the four principles of

energy management for yourself? Could you come up with a couple of guidelines for yourself for each principle?

Establish your energy rituals: Choose one thing that you think will shift the needle most for you, and commit to doing it at least five times per week. This might be five minutes of meditation, or getting up without pressing snooze. Whatever it is, make it challenging enough to have an impact, but easy enough to achieve. Momentum is the greatest motivator.

Moving on mindfully

Remember, as I shared in Chapter 4, 'Accept', sometimes a simple mindset reframe can transform your viewpoint and open a new path. If you're struggling with any of this, a helpful step can be gaining another perspective. Have a conversation with trusted friends who know you well, and see if you can challenge some of the beliefs that are keeping you stuck. Start with a small move and remember, energy flows where attention goes.

8

Making sense and moving on

'Only pack what you can carry.'

John Clarke

As we slowly gain both distance and valuable perspective from the beginnings of the pandemic, we're left to consider a central question: how do we make sense of where we are and move on?

It's as though we're emotionally dusting off our shoulders as we walk away from the train wreck while at the same time scanning the horizon for another train that can get us back on track in the same direction.

In a way, everything is up for grabs – our routines and the very foundations of our economic, social and institutional systems. With uncertainty becoming the new normal, many people find themselves searching for a new sense of purpose in their personal and professional lives.

What's next?

In September 2024, I interviewed Jamie Miller, a scholar and practitioner of ecological resilience, who provides a powerful framework for understanding how disruption, when viewed through the lens of nature, can be seen not as a loss, but as an opportunity. Miller is focused on the application of biomimicry, and his perspective on resilience teaches us that in moments of upheaval, like those we've experienced during the pandemic, we are presented with the chance to reorganise, innovate and find new meaning.

Ecological resilience versus engineering resilience

One of the most profound ideas Miller explores is the difference between ecological resilience and engineering resilience. In engineering, resilience is about maintaining stability – building structures that resist change and withstand external pressures. Think of a building designed to stay strong and withstand 100-year storm events. The goal in engineering resilience is to preserve the original state, even if external conditions shift.

Miller contrasts this with ecological resilience, which is the capacity to adapt and thrive in the face of change.

> Ecological resilience is about adapting to change. Nature does that through multiple levels of adaptations, based on continual feedback loops and change. Before the pandemic, many aspects of society functioned with a mindset akin to engineering resilience. Our workplaces, economies and institutions were built to resist disruption, to keep things running smoothly and predictably. But as we saw, these systems were

not as robust as they seemed. The pandemic acted as a destabilising force, revealing the fragility of many societal structures.

Miller uses the analogy of a cube and a ball in a bowl of water to explain this concept. The cube represents engineering resilience, staying static as the water moves around it. But when the water becomes turbulent, the cube jerks around violently, unable to cope with the changing environment. Ecological resilience, on the other hand, is represented by the ball, which moves fluidly with the water, adapting harmoniously to the changes around it.

As we reflect on how society was and continues to be impacted by the pandemic, it's clear that many of our structures were designed like cubes, trying to stay stable in the face of immense change. But the pandemic showed us that rigid systems aren't always the most resilient. Instead, we need to become more like the ball, embracing adaptability and fluidity.

Safe-fail versus fail-safe

One of the key lessons Miller draws from nature is the concept of safe-fail versus fail-safe. In human systems, we often strive to avoid failure at all costs, building fail-safe mechanisms into our processes to ensure that nothing goes wrong. However, nature operates differently. In natural systems, failure is not something to be feared; it is embraced as a critical part of growth and adaptation.

Miller explains, 'In nature, there's no such thing as fail-safe. Instead, we see safe-fail systems, where small failures contribute to learning and resilience.' In nature, organisms and ecosystems are constantly experimenting, making small adjustments, and learning from failures to evolve and survive.

This perspective is particularly relevant when we think about how society responded to the pandemic. We were thrust into a situation where small failures were inevitable – whether in healthcare, education or the workplace. But instead of viewing these failures as catastrophic, we can choose to see them as opportunities for improvement. The rapid shift to remote work, the rethinking of supply chains and the emphasis on mental health were all examples of small adaptations that, while challenging, provided valuable lessons for the future.

By embracing failure as a part of the process, we can learn to navigate disruption with resilience. Rather than resisting change or fearing failure, we can approach it with curiosity, seeing each challenge as a stepping stone to innovation and growth.

The adaptive cycle: a model for growth

One of the most powerful concepts Miller leverages is the adaptive cycle, a model from ecology that describes how systems go through phases of growth, conservation, release and reorganisation. In nature, these cycles are continuous. For example, a forest grows, matures, experiences a fire (release), and then regenerates in a new form (reorganisation).

'Whenever there's a release in nature, there's a reorganisation. It's a reset, an opportunity to rebalance with the environment,' says Miller. This adaptive cycle offers a powerful metaphor for how society can find meaning in the post-pandemic world. The pandemic was a release – a disruption that forced a break from the past. But this period of release is also a chance to reorganise and build something better.

This adaptive cycle mirrors the principles I explore in my own work: engage, accept, activate and release. These are the same principles that can guide us as we navigate the post-pandemic world. We need to engage with the signals of change, accept that things are different, activate our optimism and energy for the future, and release the things that no longer serve us.

The pandemic has given us the opportunity to rethink our values and how we want to live. It has allowed us to ask fundamental questions about the way we work, the importance of community and the need for sustainability. Like a forest regenerating after a fire, we are now in the reorganisation phase, where we have – perhaps for the first time in our lives – to rethink how we go about building our own, more resilient ecosystem.

Finding meaning through resilience

In the end, finding meaning where we are is about more than just returning to normal. It's about embracing what's different about our lives, learning from disruption, and using this moment as an opportunity to create something better. Miller reminds us that nature is the most beautiful example of resilience. It's been around much longer than us – 3.8 billion years. Humans have just arrived, and nature will survive with or without us.

As we move forward, we can take these lessons from nature and apply them to our own lives and systems. By adopting the principles of ecological resilience, we can find meaning in where we are – not by clinging to the past, but by adapting, learning and evolving. This is how we find purpose in a world that is constantly changing; not by resisting disruption, but by embracing it as an opportunity for growth.

The human side of leadership – what do we do now?

As Jamie Miller's framework shows, society needs to embrace change as nature does, flowing with disruption rather than resisting it. But once we understand this at a systemic level, the next question becomes: how do leaders embody and guide this adaptability on a personal level? How do leaders, in their day-to-day work, move from theory into practice?

This is where Shamal Dass's leadership philosophy comes into play, providing a deeply human angle on the way leaders can navigate the complexity of a post-pandemic world. Reflecting on decades of executive and board roles, Dass, an adjunct associate professor at the UNSW Business School, contends that leadership is not about exerting power or making 'brilliant' decisions in isolation – his core message is simple, but profound: leadership is fundamentally about *relationships, trust and understanding your own story*. In an era where complexity and disruption are the norm, Dass believes that leadership cannot be about control – it must be about connection.

Start with your personal narrative

Dass is unapologetic about the fundamentals of effective leadership. 'If you have an average-performing team,' he tells me in a

2024 interview, 'you're probably not a great leader.' He believes that having clarity on your personal narrative – knowing your values, motivations and what drives you – is crucial for connecting with others. 'Unless in your head and your heart you know what you're about,' he says, 'you cannot connect with anyone else. What I think a lot of leaders lack is a narrative about why they're there personally. If you can't tell anyone around you that story, then you can't lead them.'

For leaders today, this means going beyond the surface level activities of management and engaging in deeper reflection about who they are and what they stand for. Dass urges leaders to spend time identifying their core purpose. This doesn't have to be a grandiose mission to change the world; it can be something as simple as leading with a commitment to family values, or creating a supportive work environment. The point is that without this clarity, leaders will struggle to inspire others or build meaningful connections. Leadership, at its core, is about influence. But to influence others, you need to be aligned with your own story; this alignment is a conduit to trust.

'Trust is the foundation of any effective relationship, and leadership is no exception,' says Dass. He is clear on the point that leadership is relational, not transactional. It's not about issuing commands or controlling outcomes, but about building genuine, trust-based relationships that motivate people to follow your lead. 'None of it is actually an exertion of overt power; it's more a covert sort of influence, and that's all relationship and trust.'

Start hiring for character over technical competence

We tend to work in a world where favouring technical skills is the default, but Dass argues that leaders need to focus more on character and maturity. While technical expertise is important, it's not enough to deliver in today's workplace. And this means we need to invest more in the process of recruitment.

'We need to hire and develop individuals who have the emotional maturity to handle change, collaborate effectively, and contribute to a positive team culture. In job descriptions, we spend so much time on technical capability, and we spend no time on character,' Dass points out. This emphasis on character is particularly relevant in times of disruption, when emotional intelligence becomes critical for maintaining team cohesion and morale. Leaders who prioritise character alongside skills will build better equipped, resilient teams that can adapt to change and manage uncertainty. 'Facing the current complex environment,' he says, 'I don't need more technical people in my team; I need people who can challenge us and bring a different dimension.'

Dass walked his talk recently, when he onboarded a candidate based on their unique lived experience, career pathway and relational maturity – in short, someone with the ability to bring a fresh, diverse perspective to the team. Dass admits that this decision made the orientation process bumpy, since the candidate did not fit the mould of the elite, privileged, male-dominated investment management industry. However, he was confident that this person's character would elevate the team in the long run, since they could offer a different perspective and rethink how the business creates value for clients and the community. His point is clear: technical skills can be learned, but character traits like integrity, curiosity, patience, adaptability and the ability to think differently and form connections are far more valuable in building resilient, forward-thinking teams.

Use meetings for coaching, not activity updates

In addition to knowing their own story and building trust, leaders must also be willing to engage in ongoing feedback and reflection. This is another area where Dass's approach aligns with modern leadership principles. He encourages leaders to move beyond surface-level activities like task management and focus on deeper, reflective conversations with their teams. These conversations allow leaders to provide valuable feedback, offer support and help their team members grow both personally and professionally.

Dass advocates for shifting the focus of one-on-one meetings from activity updates to coaching and reflection. 'Most one-on-ones are actually coaching, not activity updates. What did you do? How did that feel? Was it a good experience for the client? Is there anything you would have changed in the process? Why do you think you reacted that way to that email/discussion/feedback?' This reflective approach encourages team members to think critically about their work, learn from their experiences and continuously improve. It also allows leaders to offer guidance and support in a way that fosters growth and development rather than simply helping team members manage tasks.

Critical thinking: the next real superpower

As I mentioned in the Introduction to this book, there is no more dangerous time to be neutral on change. The warning applies especially to being neutral on technology, as we see profound advancements in artificial intelligence. This is no time to be a bystander to AI. As it begins to understand and manipulate human emotions, thoughts and behaviours, individuals are at risk of losing control over their choices and identities. This is where critical thinking becomes crucial.

The role of critical thinking is a theme in the work of bestselling author Yuval Noah Harari, who makes a clear and simple argument in his 2018 book, *21 Lessons for the 21st Century*: technology isn't necessarily bad, but you need to know what you want it to help you with. If you're not clear on this, then technology will decide for you. Harari warns that AI and data-driven algorithms might know us better than we know ourselves, using data to predict and influence decisions, from what we purchase to how we vote.

To counter this, Harari stresses the need for critical thinking as a defence against manipulation. He argues that individuals must question their own biases, challenge the information presented to them, and be aware of how their decisions are being influenced by unseen forces. In a world where technology shapes our realities, critical thinking is key to maintaining personal autonomy. Without it, we risk becoming passive participants in a system where decisions are increasingly made for us by algorithms. For Harari, developing the ability to critically evaluate information, question intentions and reflect on our own choices is crucial for safeguarding freedom in this tech-driven age.

Whether it's evaluating the promises and pitfalls of AI, navigating ethical dilemmas or sifting through endless streams of data, critical thinking forces us to slow down, engage our minds and demand better answers. In an age where the lines between real and artificial, right and wrong, true and false are increasingly blurred, exercising critical thinking is no longer optional – it's absolutely fundamental to moving forward intelligently and responsibly.

Critical thinking and artificial intelligence
Sami Mäkeläinen, an internationally experienced foresight professional, is a standout voice on the very noisy subject of AI, routinely bringing a reality check into the crowded mix of opinions on this rapidly moving tech tool.

'Most of what we hear about AI is already outdated, and anyone claiming to understand it fully is kidding themselves,' he says. 'The rapid evolution of AI, especially generative AI, means that by the time research or analysis is published, it's already behind.'

He points out that both technologists and academics struggle with this fast pace, while corporates impatiently demand a return on investment, not realising that meaningful research takes time. Mäkeläinen's message is simple: stop relying on outdated information and embrace the fact that we don't know everything.

The natural temptation in a situation like this is to cling to simple, comforting explanations. We want clarity. We want definitive answers about what AI can and can't do. But here's the hard truth: we need to get comfortable with the unknown. Critical thinking involves resisting the urge to settle for easy answers and instead asking tougher questions, even when the answers are incomplete.

You don't need to know how AI works – but you do need to know how to use it

One of the biggest misconceptions about AI is that you need to understand its inner workings to use it effectively. People often feel pressured to learn the technical details of machine learning models, neural networks and algorithmic processes. But Mäkeläinen offers much-needed counsel: 'It's pointless to try to learn exactly how the technology works – what we *can* do is learn to use it effectively.'

This is a crucial distinction. Trying to fully understand AI's mechanics is like trying to memorise every detail of how a car engine works before driving. You don't need that depth of technical knowledge to operate a car, and you don't need it to work with AI either. The key is in learning how to apply AI in your specific context. The real power of AI isn't in understanding every algorithmic detail, but in knowing how to use the tool to solve real-world problems.

Mäkeläinen has an analogy to illustrate this point: most people can't explain how a bicycle works, but that doesn't stop them from riding one without falling off. The same applies to AI. You don't need to get lost in the weeds of technical jargon;

you need to focus on how AI can support your specific tasks, projects and challenges. This is where critical thinking comes into play – knowing how to apply a tool effectively, even if you don't fully understand its inner workings, is a key skill in the modern knowledge economy.

AI as your intern

Mäkeläinen offers an incredibly useful metaphor for thinking about AI: 'It's useful to think of the current GenAI systems as interns – highly intelligent, fresh out of university, very eager to help you, but with no real-world experience.' This metaphor serves as a reminder that while AI can be powerful and efficient, it's not a flawless, omnipotent force. Like a new intern, it's smart and capable, but prone to errors and lacking the experience to make nuanced decisions.

This perspective shifts the responsibility back to the user – you, the knowledge worker. Just as you wouldn't hand over critical decisions to a fresh intern without overseeing them, you shouldn't blindly trust AI outputs without applying your own judgement and expertise. Critical thinking requires that you see AI for what it is: a tool that can assist, streamline and even enhance your work, but one that should not operate without human guidance. In fact, you'll need to teach AI how to best serve your needs, just like you would any eager but inexperienced new hire.

This also means the role of critical thinking will evolve as AI evolves. Right now, AI might function like an intern, but as it develops it might become more akin to a highly educated assistant or even a domain expert in certain areas. By 2025 or 2026, Mäkeläinen speculates, AI might be 'more of a PhD student of everything'. As the technology advances, the metaphors we use to understand it will need to evolve as well. Critical thinking helps us stay flexible, recognising that while AI will grow more powerful, it will always require human judgement to guide its application.

Ethical complexities and the 'best available human' guideline

Of course, no discussion of AI would be complete without addressing its ethical implications. Mäkeläinen acknowledges the ethical complexities inherent in using AI, noting that while many concerns are valid, some are overblown. He proposes a practical way of navigating these dilemmas through what he calls the 'best available human' heuristic.

Here's how it works: whenever you're faced with a task or problem, ask yourself, 'Who is the best available human I can lean on for help?' Then compare that to the best available AI for that same task. If AI turns out to be better than the best available human in that particular context, Mäkeläinen sees no reason to avoid using AI. 'If the best available AI for that particular question at that particular time in that particular context turns out to be better than the best available human, I have no qualms about turning to an AI instead.'

This is a brilliant application of critical thinking in real-world decision-making. It encourages knowledge workers to assess AI on a case-by-case basis, rather than being swept away by the broader ethical debates around it. It's about context – understanding when AI can add value and when human expertise is still the better option. Critical thinking means using the best tool for the job, whether that's AI or a human colleague.

If you have a computer, you have access to the same AI as Bill Gates

One of the most revolutionary aspects of AI, according to Mäkeläinen, is its accessibility. Unlike previous technological advancements, which required significant financial investment to access, AI is now available to anyone with a relatively small monthly subscription. 'There is no amount of money in the world that will buy you access to a better model than anyone on the planet with twenty dollars per month to spare has access to,' Mäkeläinen says.

This democratisation of AI is a game-changer for knowledge workers. It means that you have access to the same tools as some of the world's largest companies and the most advanced research institutions. But access alone isn't enough – you need to approach AI with curiosity and a willingness to learn through experimentation. Mäkeläinen urges people to engage with AI directly, using it not just as an 'answer engine', but as a learning tool.

This shift from using AI to get answers to using AI to generate questions is critical. 'AI excels at quizzing you on a topic and providing immediate constructive feedback,' Mäkeläinen explains. This makes AI a powerful tool for self-directed learning. Critical thinking here means recognising that AI isn't just there to give you the right answer – it can help you refine your questions, test your assumptions and guide your learning process.

Moving forward: critical thinking as your superpower

The bottom line? In an AI-driven world, critical thinking is your superpower. AI tools are becoming more powerful, accessible and pervasive, but it's up to you to engage with them intelligently. Mäkeläinen makes it clear that knowledge workers who embrace critical thinking – who question assumptions, test their ideas and adapt to new information – will be the ones who thrive in this new landscape.

But this isn't just about using AI effectively – it's about staying ahead of the curve. The only way to truly understand the cutting edge of AI is to 'go there yourself and use the tools'. Don't rely on outdated information, and don't fall into the trap of overestimating your understanding. Instead, approach AI with a mindset of continuous learning and adaptability.

In a world where AI is evolving faster than any one person or organisation can fully comprehend, the ability to think critically – to question, evaluate and apply AI tools in a meaningful way – will set you apart. AI might be the tool of the future, but critical thinking will always be what powers that tool effectively.

For knowledge workers, and anyone using AI, this means one thing: embrace the technology, but never stop thinking for yourself.

Conclusion

True north versus magnetic north

*'The measure of intelligence is the
ability to change.'*

Albert Einstein

In the Introduction, I wrote about how the workplace feels today – disordered and messy, with professional boundaries that are constantly moving. The uncertainty around the new rules of engagement is making us nervous – so nervous that many of us are quietly stepping back to a safe place, and some of us are locking the door behind us. And what we're losing as we move into that safe place is of real concern: the opportunity to exercise creative leadership, promote innovation, and prepare and adapt to what's coming next. Leaders tell me privately they're 'done with leading', or that they've 'totally changed the way they lead' by drastically dialling back their opinions.

What's next?

What I wanted to offer up are ways to unlock the door and step into an active conversation with change, to have a voice in how we want to reorder the way we work and live. To be deliberate about how change plays out, so we don't end up on a default setting, in someone else's version of the future.

If you have run any of the high-AQ habits mentioned through this book, then you have already accepted an invitation to move from reacting and responding to change, to anticipating and influencing it. And as we consider how to define the practice of modern leadership, and what exactly is required of us, I believe that this is what we need more of: more people who are active players in change; more learners willing to adopt a mindset that is fit for purpose in today's world; leaders and learners exercising an expanded definition of how to adapt.

The 'engage, accept, activate, release' model is not a reaction to the chaos of the world we find ourselves in – it's a way of thinking that can help us collect ourselves in the cycle and ground us in a new sense of calm. It's a challenge to bring more order to our day; to use our imagination and strengthen our sense of personal agency. And most importantly, to co-create a future that is intentional and not accidental by changing our behaviour in the present. The fundamentals of this book are anchored in adaptability, but they also tap into the fascinating basics of 'futures thinking', a field of study that helps us explore, imagine and prepare for multiple possible futures, to make better decisions in the present.

Conclusion

The closer we are to change, the more resilient we are

Through my many conversations with corporate leaders for this book, there is one observation that became increasingly clear: the closer we are to change, the more resilient we are.

One Sydney-based transformation expert told me that resilience is this simple. Resilience is a doing word. He shared with me that the data across his large-scale organisation tells an undeniable story – the closer his people are to the pace and scale of change, the more resilient they are. They're rehearsing change every day, in a continual process of absorbing and negotiating change. Their colleagues sitting 25 floors above them in more central and strategic teams, who have less interaction with frontline change, are simply less agile, less mentally flexible and less efficient in moving with shifting dynamics.

The fundamental lesson of this observation is a powerful one. As we think about where we place ourselves every day – and the way we design our jobs, recruit and retain talent – we need to be clear that the traits that are single-handedly determining success are competencies not found on any formal curriculum: flexible mindset, optimism, positivity, and a 'can do' attitude. As leadership expert Adam Grant says: 'In the past, people were hired and promoted based on ability. In the future, the more valuable currency will be agility. We should bet on people with the motivation to learn and the flexibility to change.'

The objective of this book is simple: to help you move from ability to agility. To move from reacting and responding to change, to anticipating and influencing change. To avoid waiting for change to happen, and instead, step into the slipstream of change, pre-empt what is coming next, and shape the way it lands around you.

If you are a knowledge worker with some degree of freedom to organise yourself around change, this book is primarily for you. I hope this frees you up and empowers you to lift others who don't have the privileges attached to this segment of the population, because upgrading our AQ is not only for highly skilled workers, but also for anyone wanting to create a *preferred* future for themselves – not one that is simply projected or possible. This simple but seismic shift in our mindset requires us to be in a continual conversation with what is changing, both around us and within us. This takes time, energy and a degree of personal agency. You may not have the space for it today. But if you can find fifteen minutes, try to run one high-AQ habit, start there and see what comes of it.

As discussed in the previous chapters, this involves four principles:
1. **Engage** with the signals of change.
2. **Accept** what's changing, both around us and within us.
3. **Activate** our optimism for the new.
4. **Release** what's holding us back.

Adapting is a commitment to changing well

While the future of work looks different for all of us, the fundamental leadership skill that will set you apart is the same:

adaptability. This standalone trait, which will continue to define great leaders, has an expanded definition in a more demanding world and workplace. As we take on both the rapid and gradual processes of change in parallel, the greatest decision we can make is the one that allows us to adopt a mindset that is aligned with the world we find ourselves in today. We need to meet ourselves where we are: managing the chaos of a household in between school drop-off and pick-up, juggling multiple jobs, dealing with the increased cost of living. The list is endless, but the pay-off of paying attention to building AQ is transformative. It's a life of feeling more in control, more fulfilled, happier and healthier.

Being more adaptable isn't about ploughing forward blindly; it's about moving forward with intention. And sometimes that means creating a pause, our own version of a 'biodome', a protected place where we can slow down and recalibrate. We need to give ourselves – and our teams – the room to observe, rethink and find a path forward that's rooted in what we truly need, not just what we've always done. As Alina Costache says, 'Without that, all the policies we put in place are just going to be gimmicks.'

Adaptability, then, is not a rush to change; it's a commitment to changing well.

To change well, we need to create space. If we can find space to reflect in the quiet moments of our day, we can start to embed high-AQ habits into our thinking. When people tell me they have no energy for change, I respond with a question that I'm constantly asking myself: how much time do you spend aimlessly scrolling on your phone every day? If you're looking for a place to start, a way to create a small space in your day to build your AQ, this is it. In just fifteen minutes a day, you can do something that has an actual return on investment, and free up headspace to consider a new way to move forward.

Highly adaptable people are happier people

When I think about the top three people in my life who are truly energising to be around, they each have high AQ in common. They can read a room, they can read the market, and they start actively leading themselves when others around them are losing their way dealing with the same changes. I've watched each of them make tough career calls, respectfully exit teams and upskill rapidly in new tech, years before their colleagues. These are people with huge family commitments and heavy schedules. I'm continually inspired by their endurance, their generosity in lifting others up along the way, their consistently upbeat tone and their enduring sense of optimism.

They may visit the waiting place, but they never unpack. They use it as a place to regenerate, to regroup and prepare for a new route. Even when they're figuring things out, they're very social and are constantly connecting with people, working hard on maintaining their friendships. And they can always identify what's coming next, and voluntarily interrupt their path where necessary to innovate themselves.

This is the kind of savvy pragmatism we need to reach for – a readiness to redirect ourselves, even if it's in the smallest of ways.

Because even the small moves we make in a long game will help us make progress towards a better place for ourselves and others. When direction is more important than speed, then the slightest shift on the life compass is a start. Making small moves is in itself a high-AQ habit and illustrates the kind of initiative and attitude that will preserve our relevance well into the 2020s and beyond. This characteristic of savvy pragmatism has propelled other generations through equally uncertain times. As my friend and leading social demographer Bernard Salt tells me, 'Savvy pragmatism supported by a generous dollop of optimism goes a long way to carving out a way forward when others can merely see obstacles. Never give up. Never look for comfort in negativism. The best way forward and sometimes the only way forward is to create a pathway by your own determination.' The Stockdale paradox is another good example of this type of pragmatism: a willingness to balance a clear-eyed view of our reality with a deep, unshakable belief that we will eventually make it through.

Magnetic north versus true north

If you feel a deep sense of purpose in your life, you may have used the term 'true north' to describe that pull. The term 'true north' refers to the Earth's fixed geographic North Pole, a constant point for navigation. Unlike magnetic north, which moves around due to the Earth's shifting magnetic field, true north doesn't change. Over time, 'true north' also took on symbolic meaning, representing a reliable guiding principle or an ultimate goal in personal and professional contexts.

What's next?

I share this because in an age rife with distractions, opinions and outdated social norms, there has never been a more dangerous time to be neutral on our own true north. We need to exercise a firm sense of personal agency to sideline the noise. We need to find ways to simplify the busyness of life and connect with ourselves, to align with what feels true to who we are and be a walking example of the values that anchor us to our highest good.

In a way, this book is a plea to pause, to stand still and reflect on how you want to live. As you consider what's changing both around you and within you, through engaging, accepting, activating and releasing, I encourage you to always think about your role as an active player in change.

I'm going to conclude by posing the same question to you that my father asked of me and my sisters when we were young girls planning a school holiday: if I throw a map over *your* kitchen table, where is it that you want to go, and how can you be the pilot – and not the passenger – on your journey?

Acknowledgements

It's truly a gift to be surrounded by people who are both fascinating and generous with their time. In the short window I gave myself to pull this project together, I had the privilege of talking to many people who helped to refine a very simple idea: that there is a way to interpret and simplify the fundamentals of futures thinking, which is increasingly relevant to each and every one of us. So, thank you to those friends, colleagues and contributors who made themselves available to constantly kick around ideas with me and share their insights, which led to this book.

First up, thank you to Emma Rusher, a walking masterclass in getting things done while being an exceptional friend. Thank you for taking this idea to Emma Nolan and her team at Simon & Schuster Australia. To the Future Fit Learning team: Larissa Webster, Alicia Stephenson and Sally Chartres; thank you for the endless conversations exploring the leadership and life topics we love. Thank you to Dominic Price for walking the walk on how to lift others and encouraging myself and so many others to level up our leadership game.

Across a variety of time zones, I was so grateful to have had extensive conversations with Captain Richard De Crespigny, Sarah Cronin, Reanna Browne, Margaret Dekker, Barbara Harvey, Dr Catherine Ball, Kim Mills, Lisa Stephenson, Dr Simone Scovell, Rowie Webster, Craigie Macfie, Morgan Coleman, Brendan Howard, Shamal Dass, Sami Mäkeläinen, Jamie Miller, Alina Costache, Ken Christensen, Simon Kuestenmacher and the one and only Bernard Salt. I've learned so much from each of you, and I know the readers have too. And to the FutureFit Alumni, working with you across 25 global markets has taught me so much about the undeniable energy for change that is activated in all of us when we find ourselves in the same Zoom, or room, with open-hearted, like-minded learners.

Finally, thank *you*, the reader, for taking the time to explore this subject with me. Please connect with me on LinkedIn and be part of this ongoing conversation.

References

Apple. 'Accessibility: Hearing', *Apple*, https://www.apple.com/au/accessibility/hearing/. Accessed 1 September 2024.

Australian Bureau of Statistics, 'Counts of Australian Businesses, including Entries and Exits', *Australian Bureau of Statistics*, posted 20 February 2020, https://www.abs.gov.au/statistics/economy/business-indicators/counts-australian-businesses-including-entries-and-exits/jul2015-jun2019.

Australian Bureau of Statistics, 'Counts of Australian Businesses, including Entries and Exits', *Australian Bureau of Statistics*, posted 22 August 2023, https://www.abs.gov.au/statistics/economy/business-indicators/counts-australian-businesses-including-entries-and-exits/jul2019-jun2023.

Botsman, Rachel. 'It's time to update what a "good role model" really means', *Rethink with Rachel*, 2023, https://rachelbotsman.substack.com/p/its-time-to-update-what-a-good-role.

Bruckmaier, Merit, Tachtsidis, Ilias, Phan, Phong and Lavie, Nilli. 'Attention and Capacity Limits in Perception: A Cellular Metabolism Account', *Journal of Neuroscience*, vol. 40, no. 35, (2020).

Chartered Management Institute, *Effective networking for the post-Covid generation*, (2023).

Clear, James. *Atomic Habits: An Easy & Proven Way to Build Good Habits & Break Bad Ones*, Avery, (2018).

Collins, Jim. *Good to Great*, Collins Business, (2001).

Covey, Stephen. *The 7 Habits of Highly Effective People*, Free Press, (1989).

David, Susan. *Emotional Agility*, Avery, (2016).

Harari, Yuval Noah. *21 Lessons for the 21st Century*, Vintage, (2018).

Hendricks, Gay. *The Big Leap: Conquer Your Hidden Fear and Take Life to the Next Level*, HarperOne, (2009).

What's next?

Johnson, Steven. *Where Good Ideas Come From: The Natural History of Innovation*, Penguin Group, (2010).

Kashdan, Todd B and Rottenberg, Jonathan. 'Psychological Flexibility as a Fundamental Aspect of Health', *Clinical Psychology Review*, vol. 30, no. 7, (2010).

King, Marissa. *Social Chemistry: Decoding the Patterns of Human Connection*, Hodder & Stoughton, (2020).

LePera, Nicole. *How to Be the Love You Seek*, Harper, (2023).

Loehr, Jim and Schwartz, Tony. *The Power of Full Engagement: Managing Energy, Not Time, Is the Key to High Performance and Personal Renewal*, Free Press, (2003).

McCrae, James. *The Art of You: The Essential Guidebook for Reclaiming Your Creativity*, Sounds True, (2024).

Nohria, Nitin. 'As the World Shifts, So Should Leaders', *Harvard Business Review*, vol. 100, no. 4, (2022).

Polman, Paul. 'Paul Polman: About', *LinkedIn*, https://www.linkedin.com/in/paulpolman/. Accessed 2 January 2025.

Price, Dominic. 'Optimize your mindset with coach Ben Crowe', *Experts Unleashed*, (2024).

Ramsey, Dave. *The Total Money Makeover: A Proven Plan for Financial Fitness*, Thomas Nelson, (2003).

Rosa, Hartmut. *Social Acceleration: A New Theory of Modernity*, Columbia University Press, (2013).

Sandlin, Destin. 'The Backwards Brain Bicycle - Smarter Every Day 133', *YouTube*, uploaded by SmarterEveryDay, 2015, https://www.youtube.com/watch?v=MFzDaBzBlL0.

Schumpeter, Joseph. *Capitalism, Socialism, and Democracy*, Harper & Brothers, (1942).

Seuss, Dr. *Oh, the Places You'll Go!*, Random House, (1990).

SuperFriend. *2023 Indicators of a Thriving Workplace*, (2023).

Sutherland, Rory. 'Rory Sutherland on the Magic of Original Thinking', *YouTube*, uploaded by Travelport, 2022, https://www.youtube.com/watch?v=SG-iLV_NJL8.

Thurber, James. *Credos and Curios*, Harper & Row, (1962).

Unilever. *Unilever Sustainable Living Plan 2010 to 2020*, (2021).

Upwork. *Freelance Forward 2023*, (2023).

Webb, Caroline. *How to Have a Good Day: Think Bigger, Feel Better and Transform Your Working Life*, Crown, (2016).

Index

Abrahams, Robin 49
acceptance 11, 89–115, 210
   'adjacent possible', 115
   blind, avoiding 103–6
   deliberate processing before 103–6
   detecting impermanence 99–101
   'good advice' test 111–15
   high-AQ habits supporting 97–115
   imperfection, of 90–7
   kintsugi mindset 91, 92
   mono no aware 101
   pathway to growth 91–3
   pre-attentive processing 104–6
   reality, of 107–10, 171
   reframing 93–4, 189
   resilience reality check 106–11
   small, consistent steps forward 96–7
   Stockdale paradox 106, 107–10
   time to leave, recognising 95–6
   transience, of 90–7, 99–101
   upper limit theory 105–6
   values audit 97–9
   wabi-sabi 92
   'waiting place', getting out of, 94–5
   what we can/cannot change 97
activation 11, 117–39, 210
   energy for change 120
   exploration vs exploitation 123–7
   high-AQ habits supporting 123–39
   imagination 120–1
   optimism 11, 120, 123, 171
   testing the truth 127–30
   'what if' scenarios 130–9
adaptability x, 4, 11, 20, 27–30, 211
   commitment to changing well 210, 211
   defining in context 126
   ecological resilience 192–3
   expanded definition 27–9, 211
   happiness and 212–13
   quotient *see* AQ (adaptability quotient)
adaptive cycle 194–5
adaptive intelligence 28, 30
adaptive leadership 4, 107
'adjacent possible', 115
advice
   good 111–15

not seeking unnecessarily 114–15
testing 111–14
agency 25, 46, 80, 114, 120–3
alignment 5, 30
  learning plan 77
  loss of 23
  own version of success 50
  role models 156
  values audit 99
anxiety attack 169
Apple 136, 138
AQ (adaptability quotient) 4, 11, 28, 47
  high-AQ habits *see* high-AQ habits
  high-AQ leadership 25–7, 28
  high-AQ thinkers 24–5
  paying attention to building 211
  upgrading 47, 210
artificial intelligence (AI) 6, 8, 71, 92, 200–6
  access to 205
  critical thinking and 200–2, 206
  ethical complexities 204–5
  intern metaphor 203–4
  knowing how to use 202–3
  personal autonomy and 200
awareness of change 55–9
  scanning for signals 60–73

backwards bicycle experiment 145–6
balancing hope and reality 107–8
Ball, Dr Catherine 7, 84, 85, 86
Bannister, Roger 103
Barty, Ash 46–7
basic principles 11–12, 210
Beale, John 3, 4
behavioural change x
Black Lives Matter movement 27
Browne, Reanna 42, 120, 122, 127, 130
business strategy 77

change communication 20
Chapek, Bob 26–7
Character Ethic 35
character, hiring for 198–9
'chopping down trees' xi
classroom learning 79
Clear, James 180
Coleman, Morgan 31–4, 37
collaboration 135
Collins, Jim 107–8
constructive destruction 144–8
contextual intelligence 26
continual conversation with change 10, 55, 89, 117, 141
Cook, Tim 26
costs of not changing xii
Covey, Stephen 34–5
Covid pandemic 7, 16, 18, 40, 41, 51, 68, 127, 183, 191, 195
creating own future 118, 120, 210
critical thinking 200–2
  AI and 200–2, 206
crowdsourcing 143
Crowdstrike event 72
Crowe, Ben 121

Dass, Shamal 196–9
David, Susan 48
de Crespigny, Captain Richard 29
denial about change 21
disruption 5, 84, 194, 198
diversity in network 87
'do-ocracy' xiii
drivers of change 60, 77
Dunn, Dr Peter 4

ecological resilience 192–3, 195–6
ecosystems 82–4
  functional redundancy 84
Edelman, Marian Wright 103
elite athletes 182–7
emotional agility 48

Index

emotional energy 176, 180
emotional intelligence 28
empathy 27
energy awareness 172–3
energy curve 172, 173, 188
energy for change 165–89
  activating 120
  building capacity 179–81
  elite athletes 182–7
  emotional (quality) 175–6, 180
  four dimensions of 175–7
  Goldilocks Rule 180
  ideal performance equation 175–8, 188
  mental (focus) 176, 180
  optimising 178–82
  physical (quantity) 175–6, 180
  positive energy rituals 181–2, 188, 189
  spiritual (force) 177, 180
energy rituals 181–2, 188, 189
engagement 11, 55–88, 210
  high-AQ habits supporting 59–88
  learning 73–82
  networks 82–8
  signals of change 60–73, 171
engineering resilience 192–3
entropy 174–5
environmental stewardship 135
environmental sustainability 130–5
EQ (emotional quotient) 28
exploitation 123–7
exploration 123–7
  80/20 rule 126
  avoiding comfort trap 126–7
  definition 125
  diversification 126
  small moves in long game 126
  vs exploitation 123–7

failure 78, 193–4
  contributing to resilience 193
  learning from xiii, 193, 194
  safe-fail vs fail-safe 193–4
  stepping stone to success 78
  unlearning fear of 78
five Ls 156–61
flexibility 209
  psychological 6
  work styles 18, 74
Frazier, Ken 27
freelancing 74–6
fulfilment 35, 36
functional redundancy 84
future-proofing vs firefighting xiv
futures thinking 30, 120, 208

generation wellbeing 17–18
GoldCorp Challenge 141–3
'good advice' test 111–15
Grant, Adam 209
Groysberg, Boris 49

hanami 101
Harari, Yuval Noah 200, 201
Harvey, Barbara 80
Hastings, Reed 66–8
health, prioritising 167
Hendricks, Gay 105
high-AQ habits 90, 208
  acceptance, supporting 97–115
  activation, supporting 123–39
  constructive destruction 144–8
  engagement, supporting 59–88
  five Ls 156–61
  'good advice' test 111–15
  learning 73–82
  networks 82–8
  options created by 90
  release, supporting 144–61
  resilience reality check 106–11
  role models 150–6
  scanning for signals of change 60–73

scrolling back to look forward 149–50
testing the truth 127–30
'what if' scenarios 130–9
high-AQ leadership 25–7, 28
high-AQ thinkers 24–5
  change happening for, not to, 24
  habits of *see* high-AQ habits
  happiness 212–13
hope 109–10
  balancing with reality 107–10
  practical 109
  Stockdale paradox 107–10
how change happens 60, 127
Howard, Brendan 106

ideal performance equation 175–8, 188
imagination 120–1
impermanence
  acceptance of 90–7, 100–3
  detecting 99–103
  Japanese view 101
  resisting 101–2
information overload 174
innovation 27, 207
insights informing decisions 150
intellectualising change xiii
IQ (intelligence quotient) 28

Johnson, Steven 115

keeping small promises to yourself 45
King, Marissa 85
kintsugi mindset 91, 92

Landy, John 103
Lavie, Professor Nilli 174
leadership 27–8, 196–206
  character, hiring for 198–9
  critical thinking 200–2
  Dass's philosophy 196–9
  high-AQ leadership 25–7
  human side 196
  legislation and 18–19
  meaningful connections 197
  meetings, use for coaching 199
  personal narrative 196–7
  retreating into safety 8–9, 19, 207
  styles 19
  transformation of 28
  trust 197
learning 73–82
  aligned plan for 77
  always, in all ways 80
  asking questions 81
  by doing 79
  classroom 79
  competition advantage 81–2
  culture of continuous 82
  expanding ability to learn 80
  freelancers 74–6
  high-AQ habit 77–82
  knowledge workers 73
  modes of 78–9
  obsessing over 73–82
  peer-to-peer 79
  self-directed 79
  silences in conversation 81
  social 79, 80–1
  unlearning 78, 145–7
legislation protecting workers 19
LePera, Nicole 45
Loehr, Jim 175, 177
long-term thinking 134
looking back to look forward 42–3, 149–50
loss, change viewed as 21–4
  comfort zone 23
  control 22
  familiarity 23
  pride in achievements 23
  relationships 22

Index

security 22
status 22
time 24

Mager, Karl 80
magnetic north vs true north 213–14
Mäkelainen, Sämi 201–6
making sense and moving on 191–206
McEwen, Rob 141–3
meetings, use for coaching 199
mental energy (focus) 176, 180
milestones 158
    five Ls 156–61
    reflecting on 149, 159
Miller, Jamie 192–6
mindfulness 51, 177, 189
mindset 187–8, 189, 209
mono no aware 101

Netflix 65–7
networks 82–8
    differing viewpoints 87
    disruption 84
    diversity 87
    high-AQ habit 87–8
    mutualism vs symbiosis 85
    propagating 3D network 87–8
    rebuilding 84–6
new rules of engagement 15–17
Nohria, Nitin 26

objective success 49, 50
obsessing over learning 73–82
optimising energy 178–82
optimism
    activating 11, 120, 123, 171
    balancing with facts 107–8
    blind 107, 109
    unrealistic 108

pace of modern life 5–7
peer-to-peer learning 79
personal agency 25, 46, 80, 114, 120–2, 208
personal change x, 22
Phillips, Jack 55–7, 61
physical energy 175–6
planting seeds xi
Polman, Paul 130–1
positive energy rituals 181–2, 188, 189
positive mental attitude (PMA) 35
Price, Dominic 121, 156, 157
projecting forward 150
psychological flexibility 6
purposive 49

Ramsey, Dave 37
reality check 106–11, 169–71
redundancy 22, 25, 121
reframing 93–4, 189
'rejection is protection' 25
release 11, 141–61, 210
    constructive destruction 144–8
    five Ls 156–61
    high-AQ habits supporting 144–61
    rethinking role models 150–6
    scrolling back to look forward 149–50
    status attached to job 171
resilience 26–7, 192–6, 209
    ecological vs engineering 192–3
    finding meaning through 195–6
    hope grounded in 109
    kintsugi mindset 91
    reality check 106–11
    reflection 111
responses to change 20–5
    denial 21
    high-AQ thinkers 24–5
    relinquish and retreat 21–4

retreating into safety 8–9, 16, 19, 207
Rio Tinto 106
role models 150–6
  anti-role models 155–6
  best practice 152
  checklist for right 156
  good 154–5
Rosa, Hartmut 7

safe-fail vs fail-safe 193–4
safety share 106
Salt, Bernard 213
Sandlin, Destin 145
savvy pragmatism 212, 213
Schwartz, Tony 175, 177
Scovell, Dr Simone 165–7, 186
scrolling back to look forward 149–50
self-directed learning 79
self-management 171–3, 179, 188
signals of change 60–73, 171
  business 64–6
  checklist 70
  creating scanning habit 69–73
  Crowdstrike example 72
  definition 60
  emerging issues 71–2
  environment, scanning 69
  helping decision-making 68–9
  high-AQ habit of scanning for 69–73
  identifying risk 66–8
  Netflix example 65–7
  paying attention to 61–2, 89
  personal 62–4
  potentially surprising 62
  proactive stance 62
  saving and tracking 73
  scanning for 60–73
  specific 62
  strong signals 70–1
  weak signals 70
  wild cards 70, 72
small, consistent steps forward 96–7
small moves in long game 43–5, 126, 172, 177, 213
social learning 79, 80–1
spiritual energy (force) 176, 180
Stephenson, Alicia 15, 20, 157
Stephenson, Lisa 89, 93–7, 113–14, 173, 177
Stockdale, James 107–9
Stockdale paradox 106, 107–10
subjective success 49, 50
success 31–52
  definition of 30, 31–4
  failure as stepping stone to 78
  fulfilment and 35, 36
  history of 34–6
  looking back to look forward 42–3
  metrics 40–2, 49–52, 167
  myths about 36–8
  objective 49, 50, 51
  personal nature of 41
  small moves in long game 43–5
  subjective 49, 50
  who defines 34, 38–40
success myths 36–8
  happy family 38
  money 37
  productivity/achievement 37–8
  status 37
sustainability 130–5
  environmental stewardship 135
  profitability and 134–5
Sutherland, Rory 123–5

testing the truth 127–30
thinkable futures 43
time to leave, recognising 95–6
Titanic sinking 55–8
training for change 3
transformation ix

Index

acceptance as gateway to 90
from within x
transience
  acceptance of 90–7, 100–3
  detecting 99–103
  Japanese view 101
  resisting 101–2
trends 60
true north vs magnetic north 213–14
trust-based relationships 197
truth
  balancing optimism with 107–8
  testing 127–30
truth about change ix, 20
Tyzzer, Craig 47

Unilever Sustainable Living Plan 130–5
unlearning 78
  backwards bicycle experiment 145–7
  children 146–7
  constructive destruction 144–8
  fear of failure 78
  writing with opposite hand 147–8

upper limit theory 105–6

values audit 97–9

wabi-sabi 92
'waiting place' 94–5
Webb, Caroline 104–5
Webster, Rowie 182–7
'what if' scenarios 130–9
workplace
  complications 74
  declining levels of mental and physical health 17
  flexible workstyles 18, 74
  legislation protecting workers 19
  new rules of engagement 17–18, 207
  rejection of traditional workloads 17–18
  social learning 80

Yerkes-Dodson law 172
Young, Dr Peter 112

zeitgeist, seizing 26

About the author

Andrea Clarke is an award-winning author and work futurist who encourages people to be future fit for their careers. Working with top-tier organisations, Andrea's focus is on using adaptability to drive innovation, engagement and cultural change. A former television news reporter based in Washington, DC, Andrea covered major breaking news for Thomson Reuters and Al Jazeera English before working on humanitarian aid programs to rebuild Iraq and Afghanistan with USAID. Her first book, *Future Fit: How to Stay Relevant and Competitive in the Future of Work*, won the Australian Business Book of the Year award in 2019, and was a UK Business Book Awards finalist in 2020.

Photo credit: Ross Coffey